Mobile Story Making in an Age of Smartphones

Max Schleser · Marsha Berry
Editors

Mobile Story Making in an Age of Smartphones

palgrave
macmillan

Editors
Max Schleser
Department of Film and Animation
Swinburne University of Technology
Melbourne, VIC, Australia

Marsha Berry
School of Media and Communication
Royal Melbourne Institute
  of Technology
Melbourne, VIC, Australia

ISBN 978-3-319-76794-9   ISBN 978-3-319-76795-6   (eBook)
https://doi.org/10.1007/978-3-319-76795-6

Library of Congress Control Number: 2018934646

Cover illustration: © John Rawsterne/patternhead.com

Printed on acid-free paper

This Palgrave Pivot imprint is published by the registered company Springer International Publishing AG part of Springer Nature
The registered company address is: Gewerbestrasse 11, 6330 Cham, Switzerland

CONTENTS

EDITORS AND CONTRIBUTORS

About the Editors

Max Schleser is a filmmaker who explores smartphones and mobile media for creative transformation and media production. His portfolio (www.schleser.nz) includes various mobile, smartphone and pocket camera films, which are screened at film festivals, galleries and museums internationally. He is a Senior Lecturer in Film and TV at Swinburne University of Technology in Melbourne. Dr. Schleser is the Screening Director of the Mobile Innovation Network and Association's *International Mobile Innovation Screening* (www.mina.pro).

Marsha Berry is Senior Lecturer in the School of Media and Communication, RMIT University, Australia. She is an ethnographer and artist whose practice includes video, participatory art, and poetry, and is author of the book *Creating with Mobile Media* (Palgrave Macmillan 2017).

Contributors

Craig Batty is Associate Professor of Screenwriting and Creative Practice at RMIT University. He is currently HDR Director in the School of Media and Communication and supervises many Ph.D.

candidates. Craig is also Adjunct Professor at Central Queensland University and Visiting Research Fellow at the UK's Bournemouth University.

Gerda Cammaer is Associate Professor in the School of Image Arts at Ryerson University in Toronto, Canada, where she teaches in the BFA Film Program and in the MFA Program in Documentary Media. She is the co-director of the Documentary Media Research Centre (DMRC) and a film scholar, curator and filmmaker.

Caroline Campbell is a lecturer in Massey University School of Design Ngā Pae Māhutonga. In addition to contributing to the scholarship in children's literature and book history, she is an award-winning practice-led design researcher in the field of design, illustration and multimodal storytelling. Currently, Caroline is expanding her investigation into multimodal storytelling and mobile media.

Richard Chenhall is Associate Professor in Medical Anthropology in the Centre for Health Equity, University of Melbourne. He is currently working on a number of projects focusing on the health of Aboriginal and Torres Strait Islander Peoples, including substance misuse and treatment, sexual health, youth experiences, digital storytelling and the social determinants of health.

Lorenzo Dalvit is Associate Professor of Media and Cultural Studies in the School of Journalism and media Studies at Rhodes University. He specialises in ICT for development, hyperlocal media, mobile services and localisation in African languages. He is involved in various ICT-for-development initiatives and international collaborations.

Diana Maria Gallicchio Domingues is the founder and director of Art and TechnoScience Research Laboratory. She is a CNPq researcher, and senior artist/researcher of the National Program of Visiting Professors of the Ministry of Education, Capes (2010–2014). She is a senior professor at the Post-Graduate Program in Science and Technologies in Health at UnB in Gama and Ceilândia.

Vinicius Durval Dorne has a Ph.D. in Linguistics from UNESP Marília Brazil, a Master's in Language from the State University of Maringá and a Bachelor's degree in Journalism from UniCesumar. He is a professor and Researcher at the Education Department (Journalism) and works for the Graduate Program in Linguistics and Professional Master Program of Technology, Communication and Education at Federal University of Uberlandia.

Fran Edmonds is a Research Fellow in the School of Culture and Communication, University of Melbourne. Her research focuses on collaborative and participatory research methodologies and decolonising approaches to research. She is currently working on the Australian Research Council Linkage Aboriginal Young People in Victoria and Digital Storytelling project.

Michelle Evans is an Aboriginal woman originally from the Hunter Valley, NSW. She is currently a senior lecturer in leadership at Charles Sturt University, is a Fellow at Melbourne Business School and Fellow of the Research Centre for Leadership in Action at New York University.

Ridvan Firestone works across a variety of research projects at the CPHR, including investigating lung function capacity among Pacific children and examining hidden fat and the gut microbiome among Pacific women. She was awarded the HRC's Sir Thomas Davis Te Patu Kite Rangi Ariki Health Research Fellowship in 2014 to develop this intervention programme.

Larissa Hjorth is an artist, digital ethnographer and Director of the Design and Creative Practice ECP Platform at RMIT University. She was a co-founder (with Heather Horst) of the Digital Ethnography Research Centre (DERC).

Dean Keep is a researcher/artist who uses mobile media to create video and photographic works. Dean is currently a Ph.D. candidate at the ANU School of Art, Canberra, and the Course Director of the Bachelor of Screen Production at Swinburne University, Melbourne.

Patrick Kelly is a Lecturer in Media at RMIT's School of Media and Communication. He has worked as a digital producer within the film, television, online media and festival sectors for more than a decade.

Jess Kilby is an American–Australian artist and teaches into the Master of Media at RMIT University's School of Media and Communication in Melbourne, Australia. Jess holds a BA in Journalism and a BA in Political Science from Syracuse University, and an MA in Creative Technology from the University of Salford.

Tiago Franklin Rodrigues Lucena, Ph.D. is Professor and Researcher at Health Promotion Graduate Program/ICETI—Cesumar Institute of Science, Technology and Innovation working with the themes of mHealth, mobile content, IoTcare (Internet of Things and Healthcare), socially engaged art, health communication and intervention.

Scott McQuire is Professor of Media and Communications in the School of Culture and Communication, University of Melbourne. His research explores the social effects of media technologies, with particular attention to their impact on the social relations of space and time, the formation of identity and the functioning of contemporary cities.

Dave Neal is an independent researcher and media practitioner. He is the creator of *Alicewinks* (2012) and publishes on the use of vertical framing in digital media via http://www.exit109.com/~dnn/.

Ingrid Richardson teaches and researches in the field of digital media at Murdoch University, Western Australia. She has published widely in the areas of mobile media, social media, games and web-based interaction.

Miriam Ross is Senior Lecturer in the Film Programme at Victoria University of Wellington. She is the author of *South American Cinematic Culture: Policy, Production, Distribution and Exhibition* (2010) and *3D Cinema: Optical Illusions and Tactile Experiences* (2015) as well as publications on film industries, mobile media, virtual reality, stereoscopic media and film festivals.

Michael Saker is a Lecturer in Media and Communications (Digital Media) at City, University of London. He is also a Visiting Research Fellow at the Web Science Institute at the University of Southampton and Convener for the Digital Sociology Study Group, part of the British Sociological Association.

Alette Schoon, Ph.D. teaches television production and multimedia at the School of Journalism and Media Studies at Rhodes University. She has published a number of articles on the mobile and digital practices of various South African youth. Alette has a particular interest in using digital ethnography to document innovation and ingenuity among marginalised people.

Stayci Taylor is an Industry Fellow and lecturer with the Media Program in RMIT's School of Media and Communication. She is interested in the research and practice of script development, with ongoing projects as a screenwriter, script editor and story consultant.

Ana Paula Machado Velho has a Ph.D. in Communication and Semiotics at PUC-São Paulo and a Bachelor's degree in Communication (Journalism). Her research is focused on the themes of online social networks, social software and applications of communication and information technologies in healthcare and environment care.

Oli Wilson is the Associate Head of the School of Music and Creative Media Production and is the Programme Leader for Music at Massey University. His research draws on his creative practice in popular music and explores concepts relating to fandom, nostalgia and community through his involvement as keyboard player in the iconic band The Chills.

Rewa Wright is an experimental artist and academic writer who is fascinated by new practices in technology, art and science. She is currently working toward her Ph.D. in Art, Design and Media at the University of New South Wales in Sydney, where she is supported by the Australian Government Research Training Program Scholarship.

LIST OF FIGURES

CHAPTER 1

Introduction: Creative Mobile Media II—Making a Difference

Max Schleser and Marsha Berry

Abstract *Creative Mobile Media II: Making a Difference* provides an overview of the edited collection and outlines its structure in the three sections: Story-making, Making spaces and Making change. This introduction frames the book theoretically and illustrates the continuation from *Creative Mobile Media in an Age of Smartphones*. While our previous volume focused on creative projects as inspiration for debates relating to aesthetics, space and place, knowledge and stories and the self, *Creative Mobile Media II* explores how smartphones may influence to social change and can further expand the definition of creative practices relating to the field of screen media. Story-making can contribute to formulating democratic processes and equity, which are imperative to create change and challenge traditional models of media production and consumption.

Keywords Story-making · Making spaces · Making change

M. Schleser (✉)
Swinburne University of Technology, Melbourne, Australia

M. Berry
RMIT University, Melbourne, Australia

© The Author(s) 2018
M. Schleser and M. Berry (eds.), *Mobile Story Making in an Age of Smartphones*, https://doi.org/10.1007/978-3-319-76795-6_1

1

This volume outlines how story-making contributes to co-creation, co-design and co-production with "the people formerly known as the audience" (McGuinness 2016) and explores people's engagement in the process of production as more than that of pure consumers or passive agents. As media-making has moved from broadcasting channels to digital platforms, the contemporary media environment is characterised by Manovich's "media mobility" (2008, p. 203), ephemeral media (Grainge 2011) and what Jenkins labels as "spreadable media" (Jenkins 2013). The now well-established recognition of audience engagement through participatory culture is a baseline for the discussion of story-making. Digital enterprise has developed content creation strategies that embrace these developments. Here, one could point at Google's content creation guidelines (CCC—content framework: Create, Collaborate, Curate—Google Brand Lab); "rather than using video exclusively as a storytelling mechanism, think of it as a tool for story-making, in which consumers get to take part" (Larson 2015). In *Mobile AR: Creating Augmented Experiences*, David and Schleser (2013) point at the significance of participants in defining the meaning for MR (mixed-reality) works. This article also cites Danah Boyd's (Principal Researcher at Microsoft Research and the founder of Data & Society) critique of the term "user" as having drug-user associations. By means on shifting the conversation from the horizontal to a vertical plane of co-producers and co-creators, a conceptual shift takes place. Even in user-centric design and user-based storytelling the dichotomy is maintained. Through modifying the context of "the other" as opposed to the professional or amateur, creator or user, a different model of thinking and engagement is presented. Smartphones as nodes in networked media have illustrated how local networks and visual communication structures are shaped and co-produced.

While our previous volume, *Creative Mobile Media in an Age of Smartphones*, focused on creative projects as inspiration for debates relating to aesthetics, space and place, knowledge and stories and the self, *Creative Mobile Media II* explores how smartphones contribute to social change and add further nuances to the definition of creative practices related to smartphone media and screen production. Story-making can contribute towards formulating democratic processes and equity imperatives to create change and challenges traditional models of media production and consumption. This edited collection further investigates how the smartphone has been taken up for story-making and includes research fields such as children's book design, screenwriting, personal media, Aboriginal knowledge, music sharing, place-making and play, mobile virtual realities, experimental film-making, MR experiences, smartphone–spacetime, vertical video and Pasifika youth empowerment.

The chapters in this volume have been arranged according to three themes.

STORY-MAKING

Story-making can lead to self-representation and can engage twenty-first-century citizens who understand the risks of commercial and political discourses anchored within social media. According to the 90-9-1 formula (Arthur 2006; Nielsen 2006), there is a participation inequality on the internet with only 1% of people creating content, 9% editing or modifying that content and 90% viewing content without actively contributing. *Mobile Story Making in an Age of Smartphones* challenges this formula. The binary opposition of author/audience or producer/user and active/passive cannot move the conversation forward as it is framed in a traditional broadcasting model of thinking, with traditional vertical structures of media production.

In the context of design, Chapter 2 explores mobile media as a development for children's book design and illustration. In order to capture young audiences (children aged 8–10) through audio-visual means or as Campbell terms it, a "screened book", the chapter focuses on iTunes publications and multimodal storytelling.

Chapter 3 explores what a digital script development tool entails. Craig Batty and Stayci Taylor argue that digital development has the potential to offer a new language for writing screenplays. The chapter outlines the relationship between the technological changes and how this resonates in screenwriting practice and processes.

Chapter 4 illustrates how mobile story-making and Aboriginal knowledge are fused for "culture-making". The chapter describes mobile story-making in relation to the *Aboriginal young people in Victoria and Digital Storytelling* project. The collaborative and participatory method, inclusive of Aboriginal "ways of knowing, being and doing things", defines the connections to culture, representations, identity and belonging according to the story-maker's vision.

Dean Keep points at the more informal and spontaneous approach to media production and story-making. By means of considering the networked media element, Chapter 5 discusses mediated memories. In the context of story-making, Keep's reference to the "digital Wunderkammer" further develops the discourse related to personal expression in a rapidly changing new media ecology.

Marsha Berry and Jess Kilby contextualise walking as a creative practice research method through non-representational theoretical concepts. Their smartphones in combination with social media become tools for their individual dynamic and organic art practices. In Chapter 6, they present new expressive potentials in relation to the everyday realities of networked co-presence, virtual proximity and what these can mean for our everyday social activities and rituals.

MAKING SPACES

The essays in this section develop novel understandings towards space-making, exploring the prospects and opportunities of augmented reality (AR), MR, virtual realities (VR), mobile music and playing with mobile media. *Mobilarte* (Cammaer 2017) displays how mobility is seen as a creative concept, as being made on the move and made to move ones perception.

Chapter 7 examines mobile phone-oriented music sharing practices among groups of university students in the town of Madang in Papua New Guinea in 2015. The chapter draws upon the cultural politics surrounding music sharing and direction of power dynamics between youth.

Hjorth and Richardson link everyday storytelling to place and co-presence. Within this context they draw upon ludification and cartography through play workshops and games of being mobile with school children aged 7–16 years. Chapter 8 critically thinks through the possibilities of mobile play and urban futures.

Chapter 9 situates the mobile video poem *Mobilarte* (12 minutes, 2014) within the context of the Slow Media movement and mobile art. The filmmaker Gerda Cammaer summarises her production process and shaping of a visual narrative through image editing.

Michael Saker looks at hybrid reality games, in particular Pokémon GO, which became a global phenomenon in 2017 following its release in July 2016. His Chapter 10, provides a reassessment and an updated understanding of play and its connection to the ordinary space of daily life in the wider context of the "mobile movement".

Patrick Kelly discusses the use of mobile devices for AR walking trails including the production process of smartphone applications, Bluetooth Beacons and drone videography. In Chapter 11, he documents the process of creating the Tyrendarra IPA app, which was produced in collaboration with Winda Mara Aboriginal Corporation.

In Chapter 12 Rewa Wright draws on conceptual developments in mathematics and physics to propose that the smartphone's unique technical interface, which uses capacitive touch, affectively conjoins our bodies to the devices and that smartphones have become an actual place.

MAKING CHANGE

This section is concerned with how smartphones may be utilised for change. Knowledge and stories are integral when creating meaningful experiences. Through the process of story-making with smartphones, young Aboriginal people can represent "who they are and where they come from in the best way possible" (Fran et al. 2017).

Smartphones can make a difference to twenty-first-century citizens and communities around the world, as exemplified through Chapter 13 by Lorenzo Dalvit and Alette Schoon. Their chapter illustrates the potential for citizen journalism in Africa through three case studies of *The Daily Sun*'s Facebook page, which challenges the mainstream media's narrative of transformation.

Chapter 14 by Brazilian art and technology researchers Tiago Franklin Rodrigues Lucena, Ana Paula Machado Velho, Vinicius Durval Dorne and Diana Maria Gallicchio Domingues showcases how participatory design in combination with smartphones apps can be used to combat dengue, zika and chikungunya diseases, which are transmitted by *Aedes aegypti* mosquitoes in Brazil. Bringing the community to the centre of mobile media-making was an opportunity to promote a healthier environment, wellbeing and welfare.

Chapter 15 outlines developments in vertical video with Snapchat and Periscope gaining adaptation from 2015 onwards. Whether a mobile media-maker is affiliated to a professional environment or is a person with a smartphone producing content and sharing it, vertical videos are an emerging media format. Ross et al. provide a review of this dynamic development and contextualise it through software studies.

The interdisciplinary team of Dr. Ridvan Firestone (Centre for Public Health) and Max Schleser (Senior Lecturer in Film and TV) worked on Chapter 16. Firestone and Schleser reflect upon the Pasifika Youth Empowerment Program (YEP), involving youth aged 18–24 years from Wellington, New Zealand, in 2016 and 2017. The interdisciplinary research, combing public health, smartphone filmmaking and digital talanoa, uses principles of the social change model in combination creative engagement processes as a framework for empowerment. As part of the mobile story-making process, smartphone filmmaking, social media and 360° videos were utilised.

When we create, collaborate and curate, we can effect change. Jenkins describes the shift from a focus upon the digital divide discourse towards researching the opportunities for participation and development of cultural competencies and new media literacies (Jenkins et al. 2009) that mobile media enables. Smartphones not only afford access to filmmaking technology in "global villages", but also provide prospects for change: twenty-first-century citizens can make a difference.

BIBLIOGRAPHY

Arthur, C. (2006, July 20). What is the 1% rule? *The Guardian*.

Cammaer, G. (2017). *Mobilarte*. https://vimeo.com/90022219 [accessed 1 October 2017].

Grainge, P. (2011). *Ephemeral media: Transitory screen culture from television to YouTube*. London: Palgrave.

Jenkins, H. (2013). *Spreadable media: Creating value and meaning in a networked culture*. New York: NYU Press.

Jenkins, H., Purushotma, R., Weigel, M., Clinton, K., & Robison, A. (2009). *Confronting the challenges of participatory culture: Media education for the 21st century*. Cambridge: MIT Press.

Larson, K. (2015). *Building a YouTube content strategy: Lessons from Google BrandLab*. https://www.thinkwithgoogle.com/marketing-resources/building-youtube-content-strategy-lessons-from-google-brandlab/ [accessed 1 October 2017].

Manovich, L. (2008). *Software takes command*. New York: Bloomsbury.

McGuinness, P. (2016). The people formerly known as the audience: Power shift in the digital age. *Communication Research and Practice, 2*(4), 520–527.

Nielsen, J. (2006). https://www.nngroup.com/articles/participation-inequality/ [accessed 1 October 2017].

Schleser, M., & David, G. (2013, August). Mobile AR: Creating augmented experiences. *Anti-po-des Design Journal, 2*, 35–45.

PART I

Story-Making

CHAPTER 2

Multimodality and Storytelling

Caroline Campbell

Abstract In this chapter, Caroline Campbell reflects on how her creative venture into design, illustration and multimodal storytelling, which
prompted her to further investigate the screened book as an emerging
format for communicating powerful ideas to junior readers aged 8–10.
Campbell discusses how her initial exploration into multimodal storytelling for the tablet shaped the conceptual design and creative production of the self-authored case study. She explains how the knowledge
gained in designing and producing the seminal screened book *Josie and
the Whales* (2015) helped inform this multimodal work, which, while
designed for tablet reading, is conceived as a stepping stone towards
story-making for the smartphone reader.

Keywords Design · Illustration and multimodal storytelling

As a commissioned illustrator and practitioner-scholar of children's literature and book history, I have become increasingly interested in
the modes and platforms available to storytellers to entice and elicit

C. Campbell (✉)
Massey University School of Design, Wellington, New Zealand

© The Author(s) 2018
M. Schleser and M. Berry (eds.), *Mobile Story Making in an Age
of Smartphones*, https://doi.org/10.1007/978-3-319-76795-6_2

11

the reader's engagement. This interest led me recently to explore the concept of "multimodal composing" (Hull and Nelson 2005, p. 226) and W.T.J. Mitchell's argument that media proportionally combine to activate meaning-making (Mitchell 2005). My exploration as an illustrator into the field of mobile media subsequently led me to investigate modes alternative to those traditionally used in print picture books—namely image and text—to communicate powerful ideas, such as those concerned with conservation and species preservation, to readers aged 8–10. This led me to explore the semiotic potential of the image along with ambient and anthropomorphic sound to represent and communicate an ecological issue relating, though not exclusively, to Aotearoa New Zealand: Southern Ocean whaling. The result was the screened book entitled *Josie and the Whales*, first discussed in the *Journal of Creative Technologies* (Campbell 2015). While making this work, I coined the term "screened book" to capture the modes and technologies employed in its construction. The screened book is descriptive of the analogue and digital reproduction technologies used in the production of print picture books and film animation, the sequential art employed in comic book design and film animation, and the modes of image and sound employed in print and film. Further, the term references the actions of scanning, swiping and touching employed by the reader to enhance comprehension. While the latter reflect mobile media reading practices, the former are common to both print and mobile formats.

Since the 2015 iTunes publication of *Josie and the Whales*, I have continued my foray into designing screened books for use in primary schools and for reading at home.[1] Multimodal works, such as the screened book, are described as having emerged in response to changes in reading and writing, and due to radical changes in technology (Berry and Schleser 2014; Dresang 2008; Hull and Nelson 2005; Kress 2010). Moreover, such works "do not necessarily privilege linguistic forms of signification but rather draw on a variety of modalities—speech, writing, image, gesture, and sound—to create different forms of meaning" (Hull and Nelson 2005, p. 224). In this chapter, I reflect on how my initial exploration into multimodal storytelling and interactivity prompted me to develop further the screened book as an educational resource and civic tool. In discussing its construction, I will explain how this multimodal work is framed within the philosophy of deep ecology, the role of animals in popular culture, semiotics and haptic theory.[2] In discussing these influences, I will also explain how my book *Mr Trundle and the Tuna* (2017) is informed by comic book design and exploits "more than one semiotic channel [to] trigger inferences about agents" within a specifically narrated world or story-world (Herman 2010, p. 195).

Deep Ecology and the Representation of Animals

In contrast to mainstream environmentalism, deep ecology is "concerned with the metaphysics of nature, and of the relation of self to nature" (Naess, cited in Pollock and Rainwater 2005, p. 264). This self, termed the "ecological self", is rich in its embrace of all human and non-human beings co-habiting our living space (Pollock and Rainwater 2005, p. 268). In this sense, deep ecology aligns with the concept of "*kaupapa*", the set of principles that for the indigenous people of Aotearoa New Zealand, the Maori, inform their relationship with the natural world and their actions within that world. These principles (connectedness, dignity, humility, respect, reciprocity) constitute the basis for their ontology and are found woven into Maori lore, stories, songs and artefacts. Catherine Rainwater, writing about the representation of native animals and the ecological self in American art and literature, asserts that in addition to dominant systems of belief literature plays an important role in how this self is mediated, particularly to younger members of society. Consequently, Rainwater advocates that in addition to creating works that critique "the environmental status quo" authors provide readers with alternative platforms for engaging in green awareness (Pollock and Rainwater 2005, pp. 263–264). This was the motivation underpinning my shift from design-for-print to design-for-mobile media.

In contrast to *Josie and the Whales* (2015), human characters are figuratively absent from *Mr Trundle and the Tuna* (2017). Instead, their symbolic trace is visible in the industrial and commercial waste polluting the stream in which the long-finned eels known as *tuna* to Maori are swimming. This pollution is preventing them from reaching the sea in order to begin their long migration to the waters off Tonga to mate. In this modal ensemble (Bezemer and Kress 2008), the domesticated kunekune pig and hero of the tale, Mr. Trundle, assumes a role in keeping with magical realism's tropes of power, time and translocation as well as signifying the shift in cultural attitudes towards the representation of animals across a broad range of cultural platforms.[3] Further, and in keeping with deep ecology, both domesticated and wild animal species and an endangered insect signify the tension between industrialisation, in this case dairy farming, and the ecological self. In the screened book narrative, the endangered dragonfly known by Maori as *kapokapowai*, or water snatcher, is an ecological messenger, as it is in reality: its environmental presence signals clean water and a non-degraded ecosystem. Alighting on Mr. Trundle's snout, the dragonfly rouses the pig from his sleep, and, through a series of promptings, incites Mr. Trundle to come to the aid of the *tuna* and help them escape to freedom. Hence, in the design of this tale, endangered and non-endangered animal and insect characters and the stream world serve to signify the ecological self as well as the threat to that self.

MEDIUM AND THE SEMIOTICS OF IMAGE AND SOUND

Inspired by Rainwater's suggestion regarding authorship and media platforms, I decided to convey the tale of the threatened *tuna* through the semiotic modes of sequential art, sound and photographic texture. In comic book design, on which this and the seminal screened book are based, sequential art consists of a series of thematically framed and adjoined images that convey the world in which the story events take place. Through the world's design, the reader gains access to a "specific view on reality" that is contingent on a clearly defined "philosophy or visual ontology" (Lefèvre 2011, p. 16). In making *Mr Trundle and the Tuna*, this meant producing twenty-six black-line images that were then scanned and digitally coloured in a palette reminiscent of comic book design and Japanese *ukiyo-e* art. But while sequential art imagery conveys perspective, it does not necessarily convey voice, particularly within the context of mobile story-making for tablets and smartphones. So, to further enhance the story-world for the reader, and to stimulate his or her affective perception of the critical importance of the self-contained within that world, the sequential art was additionally layered with on-site-recorded and -produced sounds and photographic texture. In *Mr Trundle and the Tuna*, these auditory and textual modes operate in a way similar to comic book graphic expression and onomatopoeia. They thus not only provide the reader with a specific view of the world, but they serve to articulate the characters' inner and external dialogue in relation to that world.

In positing multimodality as the discourse of this current age, Berry and Schleser (2014), Bezemer and Kress (2008), Hull and Nelson (2005) and Kress and Van Leeuwen (2001) contend that the increasing complexity of media platforms to inform, educate and entertain has resulted in a creativity contrasting modernism's monomodal practices and vehicles of expression. These scholars, and Dick Iedema, consequently posit that this has led to the "blurring of traditional [disciplinary] boundaries" as well as the interchange between semiotic principles in cultural modes of expression and meaning-making (Iedema 2003, p. 33). Hence, in multimodal works it is "quite possible for music to encode action, or images to encode emotion", thereby enabling meaning-making "in multiple articulations" (Kress and Van Leeuwen 2001, pp. 2, 3; Hull and Nelson 2005). Consequently, in works designed for the mobile platform, modes may be so arranged as to "reinforce each other, fulfil complementary roles, or be hierarchically ordered" (Kress and Van Leeuwen 2001, p. 20).

In *Mr Trundle and the Tuna*, sequential art is argued as the primary semiotic channel—it is the first mode of representation the reader encounters in reading the tale. In contrast, sound is the secondary mode of representation due to its compositional proximity to the sequential art. In the case study, this mode comprises two non-linguistic layered soundscapes that are embedded in the sequential art and which are reader activated via a touch button icon placed in the right-hand corner of the screened book page (Fig. 2.1).

Intended to stimulate the reader's cognitive perception and comprehension of the tale, the soundscapes are designed to complement the environment and the events, states and actions depicted in the sequential art. In this sense, the modal construction of the screened book appears to support Kress and Van Leeuwen's argument regarding the hierarchical ordering of image and sound in film media. In *Mr Trundle and the Tuna*, however, the soundscapes have an additional semiotic function to their ancillary role in supporting the figurative depiction of events, one that is underpinned by arguments regarding the performance of semiotic modes in this multimodal era of divergent media languages and non-hierarchical storytelling (Bezemer and Kress 2008; Hull and Nelson 2005; Iedema 2003; Kress and Van Leeuwen 2001).

In the co-ordinated language of the screened book, both soundscapes are nuanced to evoke the story-world and the ecological self figuratively embodied in the kunekune pig protagonist, the dragonfly guide, the *tuna* and stream. Further, both soundscapes are deliberately intended to carry the inherent message of preservation into the reader's mind for subsequent use in the social construction of environmental civic mindedness. Hence the bottom-most soundscape, the ambient soundscape,

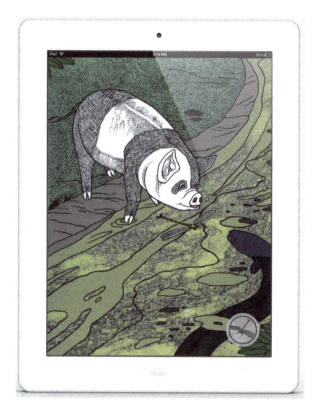

Fig. 2.1 *Mr Trundle and the Tuna* (2017), Caroline Campbell. (The placing of the touch button in the screened book page appears to privilege right-handedness, but instead confirms to the directional modality of western left-to-right reading practices)

which is designed to evoke the stream world with which the story is concerned, is a consistent thread sounding quietly and steadily throughout the narrative. The contiguous anthropomorphic soundscape, by contrast, is audibly dynamic and is intended to reinforce the non-verbalised inner states and expressive gestures of the characters. As concerns verbalised versus non-verbalised speech, Iedema asserts that "we mobilize language as sounded speech, and we further 'mean' through gestures, posture, facial expression, and other embodied resources such as physical distance, stance, movement or stasis" (Iedema 2003, p. 139).

In the screened book design, the anthropomorphic soundscape thus performs the role of diegetic speech. Conceived to articulate the human qualities and mannerisms embodied in the tale's characterisation, this modal element makes perceptible the tale's ontological perspective and values for the reader.

STORYTELLING THROUGH THE SEMIOTICS OF PHOTOGRAPHIC TEXTURE AND THE HAPTICS OF TOUCH

In further investigating multimodality to articulate the concepts of environmental protection and the ecological self, I chose to add another textual thread to the case study design and to incorporate the haptics of touch. Like Kress and Van Leeuwen (2001), Hull and Nelson (2005) contend that what makes multimodal works powerful educational tools is the affordance of different semiotic channels for distributing information. In contrast to the canonical and logocentric forms traditionally privileged in the acquisition of literacy and dissemination of knowledge, works designed for the mobile platform "draw on a variety of modalities—speech, writing, image, gesture, and sound—to create different forms of meaning" (Hull and Nelson 2005, pp. 224–225). Hull and Nelson assert further that in creating works that are applicable to a broad range of readers and that enable meaning-making across a range of cultures, design for mobile devices and tablets is all important.

In this case study, photographic texture is not merely a decorative add-on to the story-world visual representation and auditory expression. Rather, it is conceived to enhance proportionally the reader's affect, literacy and perception. Introduced at the same time as the ambient and anthropomorphic soundscapes, this semiotic mode additionally gestures to the reader the status of the freshwater ecosystem and, by correlation, the wellbeing of the ecological self with which the tale is concerned. Further, the texture, adapted and interwoven from personal photographs of weed-covered waterways, is designed to draw, subtly but powerfully, the reader's attention to the threats posed to this world as a direct consequence of human activity and industry. Thus, on one level, the texture alludes to the semiotic function of photographic subject matter in illustrating abstract concepts in print material for educational purposes. On another, the interweaving of this visually tactile mode is similar to the sensory affordances employed in silent film design, which make that media "anything but silent" (Mitchell 2005, p. 258). As applied in

Mr Trundle and the Tuna, photographic texture and the touch button, which I will discuss next, add a haptic dimension through which junior readers can sensibly appreciate the story-world under threat and thereby develop empathy for the culturally constructed characters endemic to that world.

Like *Josie and the Whales* (2015), *Mr Trundle and the Tuna* is designed for tablet reading and the haptic activities germane to mobile media and mobile media creative practice, namely, scanning, swiping and touch. Lefèvre, addressing the relationship between reading, world-making strategies and storytelling in comic book design, contends that "the reader is not just a passive agent: he or she looks at images with prior knowledge, and uses that context to make sense of visual styles" (Lefèvre 2011, p. 16). As concerns the case study, this relates to the reader's formal understanding of the tablet screen as well as his or her understanding of the actions required in activating the content composed within that screen. In this, and the seminal work, the touch button is thus a prompt. Strategically positioned at the lower right-hand corner of the screened book page, this haptic element allows the tablet reader to enter further the ecological story-world and to set the pace of the reading—the looking and listening—as desired. In doing so, *Mr Trundle and the Tuna* provides the reader with an augmented multimodal tool to acquire the environmental acuity Rainwaters contends is core to the ecological self. As regards mobile story-making in an age of smartphones, the screened book provides "finger painters" (Berry and Schleser 2014, p. 2) with an emerging format for illustration and storytelling design.

Conclusion

In concluding this case study, I maintain that storytellers have invariably been predisposed to deploying semiotic modes and media platforms that best fit the belief systems, cultural practices and values of the age, worlds and societies in which they operate. In designing works that take into account the practices, principles and values of this age of smartphone media, it is vital that storytellers interrogate modes other than those conventionally used to educate young readers about the key issues facing humanity. This was the intention behind the storytelling design of this ecologically informed multimodal work. The sequential art, the ambient and anthropomorphic soundscapes, the photographic texture and haptic elements are all intended to enhance the reader's comprehension and understanding, affect and literacy. While the issues, environment and species are specific to Aotearoa New Zealand, this wordless screened book possesses the potential to translate across cultural boundaries and communicate the need for environmental and species protection in a meaningful and accessible way.

NOTES

1. The screened book can be accessed and downloaded free of charge from https://itunes.apple.com/us/book/josie-and-the-whales/id977905931?ls=1&mt=11.
2. See, for example, C. Glotfelty and H. Fromm (eds.), 1996, *Ecocriticism Reader*, University of Georgia Press, Athens; G. Huggan and H. Tiffin, 2010, *Postcolonialism Ecocriticism: Literature, Animals, Environment*, Routledge, London and New York; A. Mangen, 2008, "Hypertext fiction reading: haptics and immersion", *Journal of Research in Reading*, vol. 31, no. 4, pp. 404–419.
3. Unique to Aotearoa New Zealand, the kunekune pig is a sociable, intelligent and affectionate breed historically associated with the country's early period of whaling, settlement and trade with indigenous people, the Maori.

REFERENCES

Berry, M., & Schleser, M. (Eds.). (2014). *Mobile media making in an age of smartphones*. New York: Palgrave Macmillan.

Bezemer, J., & Kress, G. (2008). Writing in multimodal texts: A social semiotic account of designs for learning. *Written Communication, 5*(2), 166–195.

Campbell, C. (2015). Bridging the gutter: Hybrid storytelling for digital readers. *Journal of Creative Technologies, 5*. https://ctechjournal.aut.ac.nz/paper/bridging-the-gutter-hybrid-storytelling-for-digital-readers/.

Dresang, E. T. (2008). Radical change revisited: Dynamic digital age books for youth. *Contemporary Issues in Technology and Teacher Education, 8*(3), 294–304.

Herman, D. (2010). Multimodal storytelling and identity construction in graphic narratives. In D. Schiffrin, A. De Fina, & A. Nylund (Eds.), *Telling stories: Language, narrative, and social life* (pp. 195–208). Washington, DC: Georgetown University Press.

Hull, G., & Nelson, M. E. (2005). Locating the semiotic power of multimodaltity. *Written Communication, 22*(2), 224–261.

Iedema, D. (2003). Multimodality, resemiotization: Extending the analysis of discourse as multi-semiotic practice. *Visual Communication, 2*(1), 29–57.

Kress, G. (2010). *Multimodality: A social semiotic approach to contemporary communication*. London and New York: Routledge.

Kress, G., & Van Leeuwen, T. (2001). *Multimodal discourse: The modes and media of contemporary communication*. New York: Oxford University Press.

Lefèvre, P. (2011). Some medium-specific qualities of graphic sequences. *Substance, 40*(1), 14–33.

Mitchell, W. T. J. (2005). There are no visual media. *Journal of Visual Culture, 4*(2), 257–266.

Pollock, M. S., & Rainwater, C. (Eds.). (2005). *Figuring animals: Essays on animal images in art, literature, philosophy, and popular culture*. New York: Palgrave Macmillan.

CHAPTER 3

Digital Development: Using the Smartphone to Enhance Screenwriting Practice

Craig Batty and Stayci Taylor

Abstract In his chapter "Smartphone Screenwriting: Creativity, Technology, and Screenplays-on-the-Go", Craig Batty argues that while technological advances might seemingly be breeding new types of screenwriting practice via apps and digital tools, in fact they are almost exclusively responding to market demands and facilitating existing, rather than inspiring new, practices: "every tool and app is still reliant on what the screenwriter brings to it" (Batty, p. 113, in: Berry and Schleser (eds) Mobile Media Making in an Age of Smartphones. Palgrave, New York, 2014). The question still remains: if technology can determine the type, style and form of screen media being produced (e.g. smartphone filmmaking, the web series), can it also influence the ways these works are written, beyond replicating what happens in the analogue world? How might the capabilities of mobile media shape and enhance the story-making practices of a screenwriter?

Keywords Mobile script development · Screenwriting apps

C. Batty (✉) · S. Taylor
RMIT University, Melbourne, Australia

© The Author(s) 2018
M. Schleser and M. Berry (eds.), *Mobile Story Making in an Age of Smartphones*, https://doi.org/10.1007/978-3-319-76795-6_3

This chapter focuses on the specific practice of script development to examine how the screenwriter's methods for creating content could be altered by the smartphone. Tracing the journey of a "screen idea" (Macdonald 2013) from concept to screenplay—which can comprise many documents, notes, drafts and personnel that each position the screenplay in various creative, personal and social contexts (see Conor 2013; Kerrigan and Batty 2016)—script development offers a useful lens through which to examine the screenwriting practitioner's creative process in relation to digital media devices and their potential for change. Specifically, we ask: Do smartphones and other portable devices enhance or inhibit practices of script development? Do they do anything beyond offer digital versions of what happens in the analogue world; if not, what might a digital script development tool look like?

Script Development

It is useful, first, to define *traditional* practices of script development in order that we might then understand the parameters from which we propose to extend towards *digital* practices of script development. While not always a subject of note in screenwriting and screen production research, the 2010s witnessed a swell of academic articles that define and comment upon script development. Arguably the first scholarly definition came from Peter Bloore, who suggests that "Screenplay development is the creative and industrial collaborative process in which a story idea (either an original idea or an adaptation of an existing idea, such as a play, novel, or real life event) is turned into a script; and is then repeatedly rewritten" (2012, p. 9) for the purpose of attracting funding.

Definitions can also be drawn from the screenwriting "how-to" market within which dominant industry models are iterated if not espoused. Pamela Douglas offers this definition of script development: "The process of bringing a project from concept to production; also the period when a writer works with producers to refine a script through all revision steps" (2005, p. 228). Without wanting to suggest that storytelling refinement be abandoned in the interests of spontaneity, it stands to reason that the erstwhile linear stages of script to screen might be complicated by the instantaneous nature of smartphone screenwriting (and, by association, filmmaking), therefore putting Douglas's notion of "revision steps" at odds with the emerging cultures of digital development.

If, for example, we look to screen outputs such as the web series, we find that the traditional three-step process of pre-production, production and post-production (script development is usually assimilated into the first) might in fact occur simultaneously and without hierarchical intervention, situating script development practices throughout. As Anna Kerrigan, creator of the award-winning web series *The Impossibilities* (2015–) puts it, "We didn't have to trot into any meetings with executives to sell the idea, justify casting choices, or do rewrites based on network notes" (2015). Instead, audience feedback *offered* digitally—through social media forums, tweets, hashtags, comments and likes—provides "real-world" and immediate feedback that can then *generate* story revisions, character developments and suggestions for plot and dialogue.

This is arguably one of the hallmarks of the web series: digital-relevant content for digital-savvy audiences, with digitally enabled mechanisms to garner and provide responses to viewer feedback. Or, according to web TV series expert Dan Williams, "Instead of spending a lot of time and a lot of money refining an idea that may or may not work, you can just try it out and make adjustments along the way" (2012, p. 67). But while processes of script development *for* new digital media are evolving, script development *using* the devices associated with consuming (and, in some cases, shooting and/or editing) such resulting screen works is slow to follow. In other words, smartphone filmmaking has embraced the technology in ways script development—and screenwriting more broadly—steadfastly (it seems) has not.

This is not to say that the convenience of smartphones is completely ignored by screenwriters for developing scripts. On a seemingly simplistic but surprisingly effective level, the fact that one can send oneself an email "right there, right now" via smartphones means that ideas once committed to scraps of paper can now be sent, filed away safely, put into relevant folders, and the contents later cut and pasted into other documents (e.g. a film treatment). This is what acclaimed writer and director Judd Apatow says he started doing in the year 2000, when developing the television series *Undeclared*, to keep track of ideas and influences. "Flash forward to the year 2005. Now I am a completely addicted BlackBerry user", he admits (2007, p. vi).

Writing about how the film *Knocked Up* came about, Apatow says he would email himself throughout the day with ideas and fragments of scripts, keeping them in files for ease of access later. Sharing some of these emails-to-self in his introduction to the published screenplay of

Knocked Up, Apatow (2007) shows how "in-the-moment" inspiration not only made it to the page, but also to the screen. The excerpts he shares are long and sometimes more akin to script outlines than mere fragmentary ideas, which suggests that for Apatow the smartphone was not only a useful devise to capture ideas: it was also a writing device of sorts, the BlackBerry keyboard perhaps facilitating a sense that Apatow was screenwriting "on the go".

Craig Batty's article "'Show me your slugline and I'll let you have the Firstlook': Some thoughts on today's digital screenwriting tools and apps" (2014b) tracks a course from Final Draft through to some of the more recent digital applications being used on computer, tablet and smartphone devices. He considers how individuals and teams are using these digital apps to develop scripts, whether for simple assistance with aspects such as formatting or more collaborative story-making practices such as peer feedback. Batty concludes, "With developments in technology and access to digital platforms, inspiration, ideas, collaboration and feedback can now be captured, synthesised, formatted and prototyped by the screenwriter, often in quick and adaptable ways" (2014b, p. 126), yet there have been no discernible advances in the use of smartphone apps for screenwriting or script development in professional practice.

A review of screenwriting apps for the website Indiewire suggests they can be useful insofar as they allow a writer to work on a screenplay-in-progress when away from the computer, but perhaps little else. For example, in reference to the app for Celtx, a popular rival to Final Draft, Bernstein writes: 'Billed as the number one rated scriptwriting app in the iTunes store, Celtx Script allows you to work on your script anytime, anywhere. Even better, you can sync it with your online studio [...] so you can share and discuss script changes with your team so they'll be up to date on the latest draft' (2015). In the reader comments section of the piece, users demonstrate a wariness of smartphone apps being used for this purpose: "Are their [*sic*] any apps available on Windows or Mac?" writes Debra Gordonpjul. "It is not like I'm going to sit on my iPhone and thumb a script any time soon" (cited in Bernstein 2015).

By contrast, another online review suggests that even if this were the case, few apps facilitate the writing of a screenplay by smartphone alone. The writer laments: "screenwriting apps assume that you use a desktop application for your main writing, and the app is only there for when you want to make a few notes" (screenwritingapp.com). This raises interesting questions about what a screenwriting app could look like, and, if writers are willing to use them, what purposes they might serve beyond the mimicry of books, guides, paradigms and other resources already on the market. Furthermore, if there is no discernable culture of "smartphone screenwriting" beyond what amounts to little more than digital note-taking, does it follow that the specific and often (by most definitions) collaborative practice of *script development* is likewise ignoring the possibilities offered by mobile media apps?

Towards Digital Script Development

It appears that digital (script) development—or development-by-app— has found some small traction in specific quarters. Batty notes that the app Scenetweet, developed by UK consultant and academic Stewart McKie and based on Twitter's 140-character format, promises much for a screenwriter's potential contribution to the immediacy of smartphone filmmaking, whereby the app "encourages writers to develop screenplays in 'snippets', constructing scenes 'as they go' without the need to sit in front of a computer" (2014b, p. 123). In this app, writers can also comment on each other's work, providing immediate and cyclical feedback that encourages collaborative, peer-to-peer story-making practices.

The app MyScreenplays could provide another example of where the potential for screenwriting apps resides. It allegedly offers "a novel approach to screenwriting, using the non-linear format employed by most video editors. On a small smartphone screen, this approach makes it easier to access and move elements between different sequences and scripts" (New York Film Academy, n.d.). Like Scrivener and the advanced features of Final Draft, this app provides an interactive space in which to view and assess ideas, and to move them around for comparison and reflexive action. But does it enhance screenwriting practice per se? Do the digital affordances of the app provide more than could be achieved manually?

We have pointed out that practices of screenwriting and script development appear less ready to harness smartphone and app technologies than their screen production counterparts. But perhaps, rather than focusing on this comparison, we should be looking to creative writing practices more broadly and how these might be embracing the smartphone. Take, for example, the literary genre of "flash fiction". Writing for the *Irish Times*, journalist Declan Burke (2011) notes that "ubiquitous handheld devices are also proving to be ideal content delivery systems for shorter works of fiction. [Authors believe] flash fiction to be particularly suited to the smaller devices, such as smart-phones." If the smartphone is a site of reception as well as for screenwriting/screen production, it is worth considering that works "designed to be watched on devices of many sizes have somehow brought with them the same ambivalence to standardized durations" (Taylor 2015, p. 4), perhaps even types of content. If, as Marilyn Tofler (2017) argues, the short, sometimes micro, format of web series and other screen works (e.g. six-second vines) are affecting the nature and structure of comedy (e.g. simple gags that shock and surprise), do understandings of screenwriting craft need to evolve (beyond, for instance, notions of three–or five-act structures) before truly exploiting the affordances of apps on handheld devices?

In this regard, we might look to the more specific genre of "sudden fiction" in which, according to Thomas Larson, one writes "of the immediate past, even the still corruptible present, not waiting for time to ripen or change what they know" (2007, p. 16). Writing about using this form, Romana Dalgleish notes how she is "interested in isolating moments of being; small moments that feel pivotal, moments where you feel narrative being stitched to skin" (2013, p. 3). This might chime with the aforementioned practice of Apatow: he might on the surface be using his BlackBerry to steal moments in which to capture his thoughts and ideas, but, arguably, he might in fact be reacting bodily to "in-the-moment" creative turns that become translatable and captured because of the intimate relationship he has with his hand-held device (see also Hjorth and Lim 2012).

CONCLUSION

Of post-internet poetry, Maurice Riordan writes that it is

> all too easy to mistake the outmoded for the old-fashioned, or miss the genuinely new amid the merely novel. Some of the most exciting developments will vanish, as did pneumatic post and O'Shaughnessy's Indian Telegraph. Over time the shyly inventive, the slyly subversive, or the stubbornly low-key, may thrive. We may be in prime territory, too, for a hoax. (2015)

Riordan writes in response to Charles Whalley's article (2015), which charts the shift from poets in the early millennium using the internet to source material from which to construct poems to poets engaging with websites and apps that are "more like a dynamic application than a static document, encouraging user participation and interaction". This resonates with the idea of screenwriting apps, namely that currently the market is offering "add-ons" to existing tools and software: digital versions of analogue products. And so, where could the screenwriting app go?

"As the cloud replaces the superhighway," writes Whalley, "the internet has become something that passes over us rather than something we surf over, something intervening throughout our work and social lives, something that attempts to know us better than we know ourselves" (2015). Boundaries between offline and online disappear and "as the internet flattens into reality, the novelty, fear and excitement fade" (2015). Like post-internet poetry, could screenwriting practice follow suit? What is screenwriting when practised via an app: writing, thinking, testing, developing?

In other words, what is it about analogue practices that script development processes are still holding on to? (By this, we mean everything from the to-and-fro of documents annotated with notes—by email or otherwise—to scripts printed for table reads.) Why have screenwriting apps not taken hold, unlike advances in mobile filmmaking? Why would a screenwriter or another stakeholder, such as a development executive, want to use such an app? What is in it for him or her? Given that apps that do exist almost always mirror practices that happen anyway, what is the investment, and why can we not let go? Here we might suggest that the only way *truly* to move forward—for screenwriting to embrace the digital, shaping the very fabric of what it is—is to think about apps that help writers to develop, not "write" per se. A script development app might offer opportunities to imagine, observe, capture, play and collaborate. If distinctions between author and internet are disintegrating— "a collaborator in the active, endless work of self-creation and expression […] no longer a separate place to go for information, but the medium in which we are ourselves" (Whalley 2015)—then how might a script development app provide a ubiquitous experience that connects screenwriters with their ideas, passions and feelings about story and character?

So, what are some of the ways in which writers can embrace hand-held technology to "enhance" their experiences of development? One possibility is that apps are created that facilitate virtual writing groups, where scripts are developed on an interface we might call "screenwriting-with-friends". Maybe a script development game can be used to harness and sharpen creativity, drawing on preset ideas or surrounding places and objects that are given a set of story prompts for the writer to respond to. Or perhaps the notion of "sizzlers" or "teasers"—filmed scenes, sequences or trailers of the screen work in its emergent state, used to trigger funding or create hype—can be pulled into the script development stage, using apps to attract followers and share snippets of the developing story or script.

While the viability of such ideas remains untested, this chapter has argued that digital development has the potential to offer a new language for writing screenplays and for more innovative and playful approaches to story-making. As well as leading to a deeper connection with story ideas for the practitioner and her or his audience, this might ultimately also lead to a more effective way of pitching to and collaborating with the screen industry, however that industry is conceived.

REFERENCES

Apatow, J. (2007). *Knocked up: The shooting script*. New York: Newmarket Press.

Batty, C. (2014a). Smartphone screenwriting: Creativity, technology, and screenplays-on-the-go. In M. Berry & M. Schleser (Eds.), *Mobile media making in the age of smartphones* (pp. 104–114). New York: Palgrave.

Batty, C. (2014b). 'Show me your slugline and I'll let you have the Firstlook': Some thoughts on today's digital screenwriting tools and apps. *Media International Australia, 153*, 118–127.

Bernstein, P. (2015, July 7). 7 best screenwriting apps to make life easier. *Indiewire*. Available at http://www.indiewire.com/2015/07/7-best-screenwriting-apps-to-make-life-easier-60541/ [accessed 5 June 2017].

Bloore, P. (2012). *The screenplay business: Managing creativity and script development in the film industry*. Abingdon: Routledge.

Burke, D. (2011, October 26). Flash fiction: Intense, urgent and a little explosive. *The Irish Times*. Available at https://www.irishtimes.com/culture/books/flash-fiction-intense-urgent-and-a-little-explosive-1.631904 [accessed 5 June 2017].

Conor, B. (2013). Hired hands, liars, schmucks: Histories of screenwriting work and workers in contemporary screen production. In M. Banks, S. Taylor, & R. Gill (Eds.), *Theorizing cultural work: Transforming labour in the cultural and creative industries* (pp. 44–55). London: Routledge.

Dalgleish, R. (2013). Where we're kept: Some consequences of writing sudden memoir. In *Creative Manoeuvres: Making, Saying, Being—Refereed Proceedings of the 18th Conference of Australasian Association of Writing Programs* (pp. 1–9). Available at http://www.aawp.dreamhosters.com/wp-content/uploads/2015/03/Dalgliesh2013_2.pdf [accessed 5 June 2017].

Douglas, P. (2005). *Writing the TV drama series: How to succeed as a professional writer in TV*. Studio City, CA: Michael Wiese Productions.

Hjorth, L., & Lim, S. S. (2012). Mobile intimacy in an age of affective mobile media. *Feminist Media Studies*, Special Issue: Mobile Intimacies, *12*(4), 477–484.

Kerrigan, A. (2015, May 13). 10 reasons you should make a web series (instead of an indie film). *Indiewire*. Available at http://www.indiewire.com/article/10-reasons-you-should-make-a-web-series-instead-of-an-indie-film-20150513 [accessed 5 June 2017].

Kerrigan, S., & Batty, C. (2016). Re-conceptualising screenwriting for the academy: The social, cultural and creative practice of developing a screenplay. *New Writing: The International Journal for the Practice and Theory of Creative Writing, 13*(1), 130–143.

Larson, T. (2007). *The memoir and the memoirist: Reading and writing personal narrative*. Athens: Swanlow Press/Ohio University Press.

Macdonald, I. W. (2013). *Screenwriting poetics and the screen idea*. Basingstoke: Palgrave Macmillan.

New York Film Academy. (n.d.). *Screenwriting apps*. Available at https://www.nyfa.edu/screenwriting-apps/ [accessed 5 June 2017].

Riordan, M. (2015). Editorial. *Poetry Review, 105*(2). Available at http://poetrysociety.org.uk/wp-content/uploads/2015/06/1052-editorial.pdf [accessed 12 June 2017].

Screenwritingapp.com. (n.d.). *Best screenwriting apps for iPad*. Available at http://screenwritingapp.com [accessed 5 June 2017].

Taylor, S. (2015). It's the Wild West out there: Can web series destabilise traditional notions of script development? In *What's This Space? Refereed Proceedings of the Australian Screen Production Education and Research Association Annual Conference* (pp. 1–14).

Tofler, M. (2017). Australian-made comedy online: Laughs, shock, surprise and anger. *Continuum: Journal of Media & Cultural Studies*. Available at http://www.tandfonline.com/doi/abs/10.1080/10304312.2017.1313388 [accessed 12 June 2017].

Whalley, C. (2015). Post-internet poetry. *Poetry Review, 105*(2). Available at http://postinternetpoetry.tumblr.com/post/132597769861/this-has-been-a-bluegreen-message-exiting-the [accessed 12 June 2017].

Williams, D. (2012). *Web TV series: How to make and market them*. Harpenden: Kamera.

CHAPTER 4

From the Studio to the Bush: Aboriginal Young People, Mobile Story-Making and Cultural Connections

Fran Edmonds, Richard Chenhall, Scott McQuire and Michelle Evans

Abstract Between 2014 and 2016, a group of Southeast Australian Aboriginal young people from Korin Gamadji Institute (KGI) participated in three digital storytelling workshops, learning to use a range of digital technologies to assist in creative explorations of their culture and identities. The initial workshops were conducted at the Australian Centre for the Moving Image (ACMI), where professional digital storytelling facilitators supported young participants in constructing their stories in

F. Edmonds (✉) · S. McQuire
School of Culture and Communication, University of Melbourne, Melbourne, VIC, Australia

R. Chenhall
School of Global and Population Health, University of Melbourne, Melbourne, VIC, Australia

M. Evans
School of Management and Marketing, Charles Sturt University, Sydney, NSW, Australia

© The Author(s) 2018
M. Schleser and M. Berry (eds.), *Mobile Story Making in an Age of Smartphones*, https://doi.org/10.1007/978-3-319-76795-6_4

31

a studio environment. Locating the final workshop at Camp Jungai, a place of cultural significance for Aboriginal Victorians, inspired participants' creative use of mobile devices for story production. This chapter reveals one approach for providing Aboriginal youth with the capacity to control their explorations of culture through mobile story-making, and the significance of a community-based setting.

Keywords Digital storytelling · Collaborative culture-making Indigenous knowing

Across Australia, Aboriginal young people are among the most prolific users of mobile technologies (Carlson et al. 2015). While mobile devices provide young people with unprecedented opportunities to obtain and distribute information, they also present challenges, including navigating the complex field of identity exploration in the digital realm. This chapter discusses findings from the Aboriginal Young People in Victoria and Digital Storytelling project[1] and focuses on the use of mobile devices and the importance of providing flexible, community-based and situated learning in digital storytelling workshops (Lave and Wenger 1991).

The project's participants were alumni of the Korin Gamadji Institute (KGI) at Richmond Football Club. KGI supports young, emerging Aboriginal leaders from Southeast Australia (Walsh et al. 2016). Situated learning involved participants working with Aboriginal mentors using a collaborative and participatory methodology, inclusive of Aboriginal "ways of knowing, being and doing things" (Coburn et al. 2013). The methodology focused attention on Aboriginal knowledge systems, which are holistic, interconnected and reflect the relationality between connections to Country and kinship networks, to inform and support identity and wellbeing (Moreton-Robinson and Walter 2009). Over the three workshops, intergenerational knowledge exchange was central to expanding young people's confidence in and knowledge of who they are and where they come from—their culture (Jackomos 2015). This process assisted the convergence of Aboriginal knowledge alongside the use of mobile technologies for creative media-making, actively encouraging "culture-making" (Myers 1994). Aboriginal culture was also promoted and situated within a contemporary paradigm rather than through restrictive notions of "traditional" Aboriginality (Balla 2016).

ABORIGINAL YOUNG PEOPLE AND MOBILE MEDIA-MAKING

The everyday use of mobile technology by Aboriginal young people is shifting the control and production of information further into their hands. As linguist Inge Kral observes, this occurs "away from institutional locations and non-Indigenous authorities, and young people are now initiating productive activity in ways that were previously unimaginable" (2013, p. 59). While Kral's observations concern young people in Central Australia, her findings resonate with the use of digital technology by Aboriginal youth from the southeast, where it is stimulating new ways of supporting, expanding and transmitting cultural knowledge (Edmonds et al. 2016).

Despite the benefits that mobile technologies provide for enlivened and renewed expressions of culture (de Largy Healy 2014; Deger 2017), in the southeast young people's confidence in identifying as Aboriginal is often impacted by their experiences as members of a minority group (Walsh et al. 2016). Studies continue to reveal that Aboriginal young people in the southeast face overt racism and bullying in their everyday lives, including at school, in public spaces and at social events (Priest et al. 2017). These experiences, where skin colour (i.e. light = not quite right) and outsiders' ideas of what is and is not authentic Aboriginality, continue to reinforce the myth that there are no Aboriginal people in the southeast. These attitudes reveal ongoing ignorance about Indigenous histories, including the trauma of the Stolen Generations, which continues to impact negatively on young people's mental health and wellbeing (Bodkin-Andrews and Carlson 2016).

These issues are complicated by mainstream media, which offers limited opportunities for Aboriginal young people to engage with stories and images that reflect their lived experiences. Aboriginal youth in Southeast Australia have also had fewer opportunities to participate in local media production compared to youth in Central Australia, where there is a history of participation in Indigenous media organisations. Outlets such as Warlpiri Media, Ngaanyatjarra Media and the Broadcasting for Remote Aboriginal Communities Scheme (Featherstone 2013) have allowed youth to see their Elders participating in making media as a "tool for cultural maintenance", supporting an intergenerational process of using media for cultural practice (Kral 2013, p. 54).

Diverse representations of Aboriginality are increasingly enhanced through digital media, including community productions distributed on social media sites (especially YouTube), and for southeast Aboriginal communities via a range of locally made digital stories that are stored and accessible through the Australian Centre for the Moving Image (ACMI) and available on the Culture Victoria website. New stories are emerging through the use of camera-enabled devices, challenging colonialist logic of authentic Aboriginality as "traditional" and dark-skinned. This diversity was reflected in the Digital Storytelling project.

DIGITAL STORY-MAKING

Three digital storytelling workshops (hereafter DST#1, #2, #3) were conducted between 2014 and 2016. DST#1 and #2 were held at ACMI, Melbourne, where non-Aboriginal facilitators and technicians provided training, with support from Aboriginal filmmakers and mentors. ACMI is Australia's national museum of film, TV and digital culture. It offers educational programmes about the use of filmmaking equipment and technical skills, and digital storytelling workshops. An introductory day was spent at Bunjilaka, the Aboriginal cultural centre at Museums Victoria (MV), where participants explored the collections, working with Elders and artists to gain cultural insights and inspiration. DST#3 was held at Camp Jungai in central Victoria, a place of cultural significance for many Aboriginal Victorians.

The three digital storytelling workshops were designed to provide participants with alternatives to the "classic" digital storytelling method, which focuses on producing linear autobiographical narratives, often using images retrieved from family photo albums or community archives (Hartley and McWilliam 2009). However, with the advent of Web 2.0 technologies, opportunities for using uncensored personal photographs uploaded from Facebook or other social media sites is now possible. In a pilot project, previously reported on in *Mobile Media Making in an Age of Smartphones* (Edmonds 2014), we found the autobiographical approach could limit opportunities for young people to experiment with mobile technology to conduct innovative and safe explorations of their cultural identities. Conversely, the stories produced by young people in the project discussed here offer insights into how a situated and community-based approach to creative mobile story-making, alongside an incremental skills-based approach to learning across workshops, can encourage a range of digital self-representations, alongside production of cultural knowledge.

Ten young people from KGI participated in the project. Most participants attended all three workshops. Their ages ranged from 15–18 years in the first workshop to 17–22 years in the last. This longitudinal approach provided participants, Aboriginal mentors and researchers with opportunities to learn from and reflect on each workshop, contributing ideas that would better support young people's acquisition of digital skills and cultural knowledge.

Workshops #1 and #2

DST#1 provided participants with opportunities to create individual stories in a studio-based environment. They were trained in the use of state-of-the-art 3D technology and animation software that required specific digital equipment, including Xbox cameras and desk-top computers. iPads were available at ACMI during workshop hours only. All videos were edited using Final Cut Pro in the ACMI studio. Story genres ranged from science fiction to MTV-style videos. Given the relatively complex nature of the technology used, its control remained largely with ACMI technicians and facilitators (Edmonds et al. 2016).

In DST#2, the use of mobile devices was prioritised to promote participants' agency. Working in two teams of four, all participants were provided with iPads uploaded with apps including iMovie, GarageBand and McLaren's animation, along with timelapse and digital art-making apps for use throughout the workshop and after hours. Although few of the apps were used for the two films, which were again edited on Final Cut Pro in the ACMI studio, the use of mobile devices allowed the two teams to actively control the process of creating images and sounds that reflected their collective experiences of Aboriginal stereotypes (Edmonds et al. 2016).

However, while participants acknowledged the new technological skills they acquired by working with professional facilitators, most expressed concern about the restrictive timeframe and formalised program at ACMI, where the design and facilitation catered to a "one-size-fits-all" approach (Edmonds et al. 2016). Participants felt that facilitators had limited time to learn about and connect informally with them as Aboriginal young people. This prompted our move away from the studio to a location providing more Aboriginal control. As one young woman articulated clearly in the focus group discussion following the second workshop, "having more of an Indigenous perspective [from] someone who is connected to [our] culture and has an invested interest in what we're doing for our culture" would better assist digital–cultural explorations. Despite these limitations, participants agreed that their new digital skills were transferrable outside the ACMI workshops. In addition, cultural knowledge obtained from Elders and artists at MV when exploring Aboriginal collections offered insights into seeking permissions and adhering to cultural protocols when producing material for digital distribution (Edmonds et al. 2016).

Workshop #3

DST#3 took place at Camp Jungai on Taungurung Country. The workshop demonstrated the benefits of informal, situated learning in a community-based location. It also revealed the importance of facilitating incremental digital literacy; previous workshop experiences coalesced to inform the final production of mobile-made stories. In DST#3, having Aboriginal experts as mentors rather than facilitators promoted independence and confidence in the young people. In the words of the participants, they were able to "relax" and "experiment more freely" with the technology, seeking support from mentors only when required. Gunditjmara filmmaker Tim Church, Palawa writer/performer Tammy Anderson and Taungurung Elder and artist Uncle Mick Harding provided cultural knowledge and guidance in the production of stories. For example, Uncle Mick's use of digital art-making apps to create designs reflecting his traditional Country inspired one young man to digitally manipulate his hand-drawn lizard, inscribed with linear artwork reminiscent of traditional designs from Aboriginal Victoria.

Significantly, all mentors had profiles within the Aboriginal film and arts community and could promote culture as contemporary and "cool", providing young people with opportunities to visualise their connections to culture as present and ongoing. This was expressed in the focus group discussion following DST#3, where young people offered insights about how the workshop responded to their ambitions to use technology to support their connections to culture and their capacity to share their stories.

Connections to Culture: Identity and Belonging

For most participants, opportunities to learn about, share and experience their Aboriginality with other young Aboriginal people have only been possible through programs offered by KGI. Participants stated that the convergence of digital technology and learning to create stories in a community-based environment enhanced their sense of identity and belonging. One participant said:

> [Technology is] a good way to express ourselves […] half of us had no idea about our Aboriginality before KGI contacted us […] I knew absolutely nothing before KGI. But doing this [DST workshop] as well […] gives us a way of expressing how we feel about culture and […] trying to find out about culture and […] other people's culture. (Female, age 18)

Such community-based spaces, where "competence is gained informally through observation, peer learning and teaching, fearless trial and error experimentation, and practice alongside access to mentors at pinpoint moments" (Kral 2010, p. 6), support young people's control and agency over the production of their cultural knowledge and the potential distribution of their stories in the digital realm.

Sharing Stories: Audiences and Social Media

Participants were also conscious of the scope that mobile technologies provide for others to interact with their stories. Participants recognised that they are responsible to themselves, to other Aboriginal young people and broader audiences to communicate careful and considered reflections of their cultural explorations, as one participant explained:

> it's given me the skills to be more mature about things and yeah, just put them out there in a safe way, and explore them in a safe way. (Female, age 17)

Participants also expressed ambivalence about sharing their stories online, recognising the potential for defamatory responses if posted without appropriate contextualisation. For instance:

> I think [our stories] need to be used in context […] Because people are just brutal, and even though I reckon we're strong enough to take it […] you'd get some comments and things that I wouldn't want to see. (Female, age 17)

Comments like these reflect participants' desire to control the digital distribution of their stories. Researchers have found that custom-designed mobile applications can assist the informal production of media by Aboriginal people and promote culture (Dyson and Brady 2013). To harness the uptake of mobile media by young people in this project, a digital storytelling app, What's ya Story, was developed and designed with participants to enable them to control the distribution of their stories (Edmonds et al. 2014). The What's ya Story app prototype was trialled in DST#3. One participant recognised the app as a "culturally safe space" while another acknowledged the benefits of the app to engage an intimate audience, allowing her to "feel more relaxed to let my true identity be shown … rather than, say, Facebook or Instagram where everyone can see it". These responses reveal the ambiguous and contested space that online representations present for Aboriginal young people as they mediate their digital identities (Carlson et al. 2015).

Ultimately, DST#3 confirmed that using mobile devices and apps for creating and sharing information was an essential part of participants' everyday lives and necessary for ensuring a strong cultural future, as articulated below:

> no matter what, technology's going to grow, and if we want our culture to grow we've got to jump on that [...] I know it's a traditional culture, but I think we do need to start digitizing it and sharing it. That's the only way we're going to keep it alive. (Female, age 17)

Conclusion

When Aboriginal young people are able to create and produce their stories in a supportive and community-based environment, where learning is flexible and informal, this can support Aboriginal "ways of doing things", promoting culture-making within a contemporary paradigm. Mobile devices also provide spaces that support young people's agency and digital expertise, allowing them to explore, navigate and construct their own representations of their culture and identities relatively freely. However, for those in the southeast, this can be compromised by the history of colonization, where Aboriginal youth remain a minority group and their Aboriginality is frequently contested. Additionally, few have grown up within a culture of Aboriginal media-making, and mainstream media continues to offer limited opportunities for young people to witness and engage with representations that reflect their lived realities. Assisting Aboriginal young people in the southeast to maximise the use of digital technology and acquire cultural digital literacy as tools for producing and consuming knowledge about themselves and their communities, requires approaches that account for the legacy of colonization, and provides a means for media-making that allows young people to represent who they are and where they come from in the best way possible.

NOTE

1. Australian Research Council Linkage Project (130100733).

REFERENCES

Balla, P. (2016). Sovereignty: Inalienable and intimate. In P. Balla & M. Delany (Eds.), *Sovereignty* (pp. 11–16). Melbourne: Australian Centre for Contemporary Art.

Bodkin-Andrews, G., & Carlson, B. (2016). The legacy of racism and Indigenous Australian identity within education. *Race Ethnicity and Education, 19*(4), 784–807.

Carlson, B. L., Farrelly, T., Frazer, R., & Borthwick, F. (2015). Mediating tragedy: Facebook, Aboriginal peoples and suicide. *Australasian Journal of Information Systems, 19.*

Coburn, E., Moreton-Robinson, A., Sefa Dei, G., & Stewart-Harawira, M. (2013). Unspeakable things: Indigenous research and social science. *Socio: La nourvell revue des sciences sociales, 2,* 331–348.

Davis, T., & Moreton, R. (2011). 'Working in communities, connecting with culture': Reflecting on U-matic to YouTube a national symposium celebrating three decades of Australian Indigenous community filmmaking. *Screening the Past, 31.*

de Largy Healy, J. (2014). Remediating sacred imagery on screens: Yolngu experiments with new media technology. *Australian Aboriginal Anthropology Today: Critical Perspectives from Europe.* https://actesbranly.revues.org/577.

Deger, J. (2017). Curating digital resonance. In H. A. Horst & A. Galloway (Eds.), *The Routledge companion to digital ethnography* (pp. 318–328). New York: Taylor and Francis.

Dyson, L. E., & Brady, F. (2013). A study of mobile technology in a Cape York community: Its reality today and potential for the future. In L. Ormond-Parker, A. Corn, C. Fforde, K. Obata, & S. O'Sullivan (Eds.), *Information technology and Indigenous communities* (pp. 9–26). Canberra: AIATSIS.

Edmonds, F. (2014). Digital storytelling and Aboriginal young people: An exploration of digital techology to support contemporary Koori culture. In M. Berry & M. Schleser (Eds.), *Mobile media making in an age of smartphones* (pp. 92–103). New York: Palgrave Macmillan.

Edmonds, F., Evans, M., McQuire, S., & Chenhall, R. (2016). Ethical considerations when using visual methods in digital storytelling with Aboriginal young people in southeast Australia. In D. Warr, S. Cox, M. Guillemin, & J. Waycott (Eds.), *Ethics and visual research methods: Theory, methodology, and practice* (pp. 158–170). New York: Palgrave Macmillan.

Edmonds, F., Rachinger, C., Singh, G., Chenhall, R., Arnold, M., de Souza, P., et al. (2014). *'What's ya story': The making of a digital storytelling mobile app with Aboriginal young people*. Sydney: ACCAN.

Featherstone, D. (2013). The Aboriginal invention of broadband: How Yarnangu are using ICTs in the Ngaanyatjarra lands of Western Australia. In L. Ormond-Parker et al. (Eds.), *Information technology and indigenous communities* (pp. 27–52). Canberra: AIATSIS.

Hartley, J., & McWilliam, K. (Eds.). (2009). *Story circle: Digital storytelling around the world*. Oxford: Wiley-Blackwell.

Jackomos, A. (2015). International human rights day oration linking our past with our future: How cultural rights can help shape identity and build resilience in Koori kids. *Indigenous Law Bulletin, 8*(17), 20–23.

Kral, I. (2010). *Plugged in: Remote Australian indigenous youth and digital culture* (Centre for Aboriginal Economic Policy Research (CAEPR) Working Paper, No. 69/2010).

Kral, I. (2013). The acquisition of media as cultural practice: Remote indigenous youth and new digital technologies. In L. Ormond-Parker, A. Corn, C. Fforde, K. Obata, & S. O'Sullivan (Eds.), *Information technology and indigenous communities* (pp. 53–74). Canberra: AIATSIS.

Lave, J., & Wenger, E. (1991). *Situated learning: Legitimate peripheral participation*. Cambridge [England] and New York: Cambridge University Press.

Moreton-Robinson, A., & Walter, M. (2009). Indigenous methodologies in social research. In M. Walter (Ed.), *Social research methods* (pp. 1–18). South Melbourne: Oxford University Press.

Myers, F. R. (1994). Culture-making: Performing Aboriginality at the Asia Society Gallery. *American Ethnologist, 21*(4), 679–699.

Priest, N., Thompson, L., Mackean, T., Baker, A., & Waters, E. (2017). 'Yarning up with Koori kids'—Hearing the voices of Australian urban indigenous children about their health and well-being. *Ethnicity & Health, 22*(6), 631–647.

Walsh, L., Anderson, P., Zyngier, D., Fernandes, V., & Zhang, H. (2016). *Evaluation of the Richmond Emerging Aboriginal Leadership (REAL) program* (Final Report). Melbourne: Monash University.

CHAPTER 5

Smartphones and Evocative Documentary Practices

Dean Keep

Abstract Smartphones are part of a convergence culture that is reconfiguring our relationship with media and arguably shifting our understanding of documentary practices. Smartphones may now be understood as powerful enablers that provide users with the tools and resources necessary to capture and share mediated traces of the people and places that form part of our everyday habitus. In this chapter, Dean Keep puts forward a proposition that the smartphone is more than a dynamic networked media tool; rather, it is a "digital Wunderkammer", a portable database to aid the storage and retrieval of captured moments that can be later used for the production of a wide range of documentary stories.

Keywords Evocative documentary · Smartphones · Memory · Place

Smartphones may be understood as a transformative new media technology that is changing the way people communicate in a networked digital media environment. But smartphones are much more than

D. Keep (✉)
Swinburne University of Technology, Melbourne, Australia

© The Author(s) 2018   41
M. Schleser and M. Berry (eds.), *Mobile Story Making in an Age of Smartphones*, https://doi.org/10.1007/978-3-319-76795-6_5

communication tools—they are also sophisticated portable media devices that present opportunities to capture, share and edit the mediated traces of everyday life. According to Manovich (2001, p. xv), "cinematic ways of seeing the world, of structuring time, of narrating a story, of linking one experience to the next, have become the basic means by which computer users access and interact with all cultural data".

The use of smartphones to create photographs and video content has become a routine practice as people go about the process of making and sharing the digital representations of the world around them. As observed by Germen,

> The omnipresence of smartphones as imaging devices has a strong impact on the fact that they encourage, help us to take photos in places, instances, settings, occasions we would not otherwise think of photographing. (2014, p. 307)

Whereas traditional film and photography is often defined by the technical and aesthetic conventions of the medium, it may be said that smartphones, due to their size, portability and hybrid nature, promote a more informal and spontaneous approach to media production. From self-portraits (selfies) to images of travel, food, friends and family, the smartphone is ever at hand to capture the evidence of our personal experiences.

Unlike traditional film and photographic cameras, the smartphone requires no specialised skill and provides users with a simple means of creating high-resolution digital media content. But smartphone technology is arguably doing much more than simplifying image-making processes. Smartphones are also changing our understanding of the ways that visual media can be used to construct, share and screen a wide range of personal narratives.

The ubiquitous nature of mobile media means that we now arguably live in a panopticon where smartphones with cameras are ever present. As we move through the urbanscape, we often negotiate the gaze of the roving mobile eye as the people around us use smartphones and tablet computers to capture the ebb and flow of life on the streets. As observed by Kracauer, "this flow casts its spell over the flaneur, or even creates him. The flaneur is intoxicated with life in the street" (1960, p. 72). With smartphone in hand, we are both "flaneur" (Baudrillard) and "phoneur" (Luke) as we drift through private and public spaces using smartphones to capture the mediated traces of the people, places and events that shape our day-to-day lives.

As we learn to negotiate the technological challenges of an increasingly digitised and networked media space, it may be said that our relationship with media is shifting to meet the demands of an ever-changing new media ecology. As noted by Bruns (2006, p. 271), "Media play an important part in shaping our consciousness and understanding of the world around us, as well as our place within it", and the smartphone has emerged as a powerful enabler whereby users are able to easily collect digital renderings of personal and collective experiences in the form of digital media assets that can be stored within the device, or disseminated across the networks.

Here I put forward a proposition that the smartphone is more than a dynamic networked media tool: rather, it is a "digital Wunderkammer", an archive in which we can store and retrieve mediated moments that can be later used for the production of a wide range of non-fiction stories. Adopting Nora's (1989) "Les Lieux de Mémoire" (the sites of memory) as a travelling concept, this research interrogates the role that smartphones play in the recording of personal experiences and how the media captured on our phones may be used to create digital stories that promote the revisiting of memories.

SMARTPHONE: DIGITAL STORYTELLING AND MEDIATED MEMORIES

The smartphone, with its cameras and associated media production software, can be used as a tool to capture the traces of personal experience in the form of photographs and video content. Like a digital scrapbook, the smartphone is perhaps the ultimate archiving tool; messages, website histories, social media apps and audio-visual material provide a record of our interactions in both physical and virtual spaces. Inside the digital heart of the smartphone we store tiny moments, audio-visual fragments of the world around us. But as we use smartphones to create personal histories or "micro-biographies", we are not only engaging in media production practices, but also building a library of memories.

In his essay "Between Memory and History: Les Lieux de Mémoire", Nora (1989, p. 14) notes that "the imperative of our epoch is not only to keep everything, to preserve every indicator of memory—even when we are not sure which memory is being indicated—but also to produce archives". Nora goes on to say that

> the archive has become the deliberate and calculated secretion of lost memory. It adds to life—itself often a function of its own recording—a secondary memory, a prosthesis-memory. (1989, p. 14)

But is the digital content (text messages, photos and videos etc.) that we store on our smartphones simply a way of escaping the burden of memory, or might these digital artefacts help individuals to unlock a remembrance of the people, places and events that occupy the past? I suggest that the personal photographs and videos we capture on smartphones provide artists and filmmakers with an opportunity to create innovative modes of visual storytelling that highlight the tensions that exist between history and memory.

As we use smartphones to collect the traces the everyday, we are also engaging in autobiographical practices. The photographs and videos that we take using smartphones arguably plays an important role in understanding our place within the world, both at the moment of capture and in the future. Van Dijck observes that

> Media technologies are not just a method of building up a stockpile of personal memories, but their function is concurrently formative, directive and communicative. They enable the self to grow and mature, to give meaning and direction to one's past and present. (2007, p. 171)

A case in point is a concert I attended by UK band Goldfrapp. A group of teenagers were running in and out of the theatre constantly filming each other on smartphones. To the people outside of this circle of friends, it may have appeared that these teenagers were disengaged from the musicians performing onstage, but I would argue that they were actively engaged in using smartphones consciously to curate and construct the media narratives that will inform their future memories of the event.

Could it be that the videos we capture on smartphones also invite an engagement with personal memories? To what extent are smartphones memory sites to aid the storage and retrieval of personal memories? Nora suggests that "sites of memory" are material, symbolic and functional and that even a purely material site such as an archive can become a "lieux de mémoire" "if the imagination invests it with a symbolic aura" (1989, p. 19).

So, with this statement in mind, I put forward a proposition that smartphones may be understood as "lieux de mémoire", an interactive archive where mediated moments await retrieval, to be played and replayed on the screen of the smartphone, shared across local and global networks, or remixed and reimagined as evocative narratives that extend our understanding of factual storytelling in a new media ecology.

SMARTPHONES: MEDIATED MOMENTS AND DOCUMENTARY PRACTICES

The smartphone has become the role model of technological convergence, whereby it seamlessly meshes the technology of the telephone with the language and tools of cinema and photography to create a portable networked media device that enables its users to become media content producers. Jenkins (2001, p. 1) suggests that "we are entering an era where media will be everywhere, and we will use all kinds of media in relation to one another" to construct narratives that exploit the parameters of digital media devices and communication networks. The smartphone is a one-stop shop for the planning, production and post-production of the media assets we capture throughout the day. Media content in the form of photos, videos and audio files captured on smartphones can now be easily manipulated and edited using a plethora of inexpensive or free editing applications (apps) and visual effect filters that may be downloaded to the smartphone.

Digital technologies, and in particular the smartphone, are shaping our understanding of media and reconfiguring the ways we engage with media tools and digital artifacts, therefore presenting new ways to construct, distribute and experience stories. Wood (2007, p. 48) suggests that digital technologies not only organise what we see and how it is seen, but they are also framing and expanding our understanding of narrative space. According to Keep and Berry,

> The portability and technical capabilities of mobile technologies significantly alters the user's relationship with media and creative practice, presenting new ways for film-makers to interpret and shape the ephemera of everyday experiences. (2009, p. 6)

As outlined earlier, we often engage in digital storytelling practices whereby we find ourselves using smartphones to produce digital videos of our interactions with the people that share our physical and networked spaces. According to the Forecast and Methodology 2014–2019 White Paper (Cisco 2015, n.p.) global mobile data traffic is predicted to increase tenfold between 2014 and 2019 as more and more people engage in the uploading and downloading of user-generated media content via mobile devices. Whether it be capturing photographs or video of the profound through to the banal, these digital artefacts are central to an emergent storytelling culture that exploits the potential of portable digital media devices and communication networks for the purpose of creating and sharing mediated personal moments across the internet.

Smartphones provide users with an inexpensive means of engaging in media production practices that exploit the portable nature and connectivity of the mobile phone. Smartphones, not being a conventional video camera, invite experimentation as users mesh old and new media production techniques and/or strategies to push the creative parameters of both smartphone technology and storytelling. As noted by Schleser, Wilson and Keep, "As a media practice, mobile filmmaking opens up alternative means of film production and viewing, thus creating new modes of cinematic discourse" (2013, p. 126). The smartphone arguably presents us with opportunities to liberate ourselves from the constraints and preoccupations with traditional cinema, and in particular the documentary film genre.

Bill Nichols notes that "every documentary has its own distinct voice" (2001, p. 99) and that, like every speaking voice, cinematic voices carry their own unique fingerprint or signature. I would argue that due to the highly personal and intimate nature of smartphones, the images and video captured on these devices are also imbued with a unique voice and style. Making digital media with smartphones may be understood as a spontaneous process whereby individuals are engaged in the act of capturing fragments of lived experiences. In his book *Introduction to Documentary*, Nichols proposes six modes of documentary. Of particular interest is the "Poetic Mode", which may be understood as an artistic form that places an emphasis on mood, tone and affect rather than communicating knowledge or trying to persuade the viewer (2001, p. 103). With this in mind, I embrace the term "evocative-documentary" as a way of describing non-fiction narratives that do not easily fit within the parameters of the documentary genre. For me, the term "evocative-documentary" invites a poetic turn and describes a documentary form, which draws upon Nichols' "Poetic Mode" and autobiographical practices.

Evocative-Documentary: Two Examples

Since 2005, I have been using a variety of mobile phones with built-in cameras as a tool to aid the production of photographs and video works that interrogate the relationship between portable media technology and personal forms of digital storytelling. Ranging from the considered construction of a photographic archive documenting my recovery from open-heart surgery between 2006 and 2007 through to the creation of video works that repurpose smartphone videos to explore notions of personal memory, these works exploit the technical parameters, reflexive nature and creative potential of mobile media to create evocative forms of documentary storytelling. The following two examples were made using smartphone technology.

The first example I present here is *Decombres*, which I made in 2014. The aim of this project was to repurpose and construct a digital story using existing video and text messages stored on my smartphone. In *Decombres*, its title aptly taken from the French word for rubble, the project adopts bricolage techniques as a production methodology. Working only with digital artifacts stored on my smartphone, video footage from a long-forgotten train trip to a country town and remnants of text messages form a series of conversations with a friend (2009–2014) were used as a source material to construct an experimental documentary narrative (Fig. 5.1).

Decombres is drawn from my memories of the people and places I would see as a child when my family and I travelled by car to visit my grandmother. The landscape featured in the video now seems unfamiliar to me; and as the landscape drifts past the train window, I am increasingly aware of the construction of a liminal space where my remembrance of the past is folded over the present to create and entanglement of history and memory. *Decombres* is arguably an example of an evocative documentary project that meshes factual storytelling, autobiography and smartphone technology to extend the definition of the documentary genre.

The second example is *Remembering Hiroshima* (2016), a film constructed from smartphone footage and archival images and employs cinematic techniques such as slow motion, superimposition and split screens to represent visually the temporal gaps and shifts that exist between the past and present. Part diary, part documentary, *Remembering Hiroshima* demonstrates the ways in which smartphones may be used for auto-ethnographic research while providing artists/filmmakers with the means

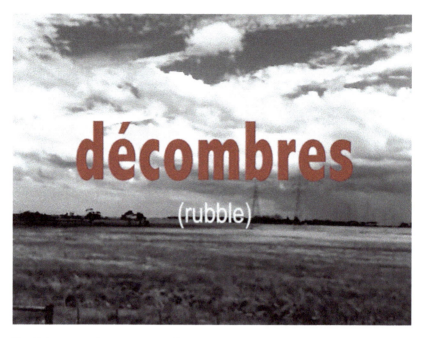

Fig. 5.1 *Decombres* (2014) production still. Dean Keep

for spontaneous and simple collection of visual data. This short film fuses digital video and analogue (archival photographs) and employs experimental narrative strategies to explore the ways in which personal memory may shape the experience and representation of place (Fig. 5.2).

Adopting an inductive methodology, I look for significant patterns and reoccurring themes emerging in my creative practice. I also adopt auto-ethnographic strategies such as using smartphones and video cameras to regularly document my personal experiences so that I can later watch the video and initiate a return to the moment in an effort to make meaning from such experiences. In a similar way to an artist making a sketch, I capture smartphone moments that I later view and assemble (edit) into video works that explore my relationship with the world.

Projects such as *Decombres* (2014) and *Remembering Hiroshima* (2016) may be viewed as examples of the ways in which smartphone technologies can be harnessed to capture and preserve the ephemera of the everyday.

Fig. 5.2 *Remembering Hiroshima* (2016) production still. Dean Keep

CONCLUSION

The smartphone has emerged as an important media device in an era dominated by convergence cultures and networked media technologies. Smartphones with cameras instigate new screen cultures and production practices whereby individuals use smartphones to capture and share personal stories in the form of photographs and videos that can be stored inside the phone or shared with others via dedicated online media platforms (YouTube, Vimeo, Flickr) and/or social media applications (Instagram, Facebook, Twitter).

The ubiquitous smartphone, being relatively cheap and accessible, presents opportunities for individuals to engage in a wide range of media production practices. Recording the traces of our personal experiences and observations has become an important form of personal expression in the "new media ecology". The intimate nature of the smartphone, being a device that is generally not shared and kept close to the body, means that the smartphone is almost always close to hand and ready to capture events as they occur.

As we capture the traces of our lives using smartphones, we are creating expansive digital archives in which to store media assets related to our personal histories and memories. This media may used to aid the production of innovative narrative forms that remix and refashion documentary practices. Smartphone technology is arguably changing our relationship with media and reconfiguring our understanding of documentary narratives and production practices and, in doing so, providing valuable opportunities for personal expression in a rapidly changing new media ecology.

In an age of smartphones, I find myself asking not what is a documentary is, but rather what a documentary might be.

References

Bruns, A. (2006). Towards produsage: Futures for user-led content production. In F. Sudweeks, H. Hrachovec, & C. Ess (Eds.), *Proceedings of the Fifth International Conference on Cultural Attitudes Towards Technology and Communication, Tartu, Estonia, June 28–July 1, 2006* (pp. 275–284). School of Information Technology, Murdoch University, Murdoch, WA.

Cisco. (2015). *Cisco visual networking index: Forecast and methodology, 2014–2019 white paper*. Retrieved from http://www.cisco.com/c/en/us/solutions/collateral/service-provider/ip-ngn-ip-next-generation-network/white_paper_c11-481360.html.

Germen, M. (2014, July 8–10). The unstoppable rise of mobile imaging and aesthetics. In *Electronic visualisation and the arts (EVA 2014)*. London.

Jenkins, H. (2001). *Convergence? I Diverge. For all the talk about convergence, multiple media will never coalesce into one supermedium.* Retrieved from http://www.technologyreview.com/article/401042/convergence-i-diverge/.

Keep, D., & Berry, M. (2009, August 23–September 1). Memories, mobiles and creative art practice. In *The 15th International Symposium on Electronic Art*. University of Ulster.

Kracauer, S. (1960). *Theory of film: The redemption of physical reality*. Oxford: Oxford University Press.

Manovich, L. (2001). *The language of new media*. Cambridge, MA: The MIT Press.

Nichols, B. (2001). *Introduction to documentary*. Indianapolis: Indiana University Press.

Nora, P. (1989). Between memory and history: Les Lieux de Memoire. *Representations, 26*(Spring), 7–24. Retrieved from http://www.staff.amu.edu.pl/~ewa/Nora,%20Between%20Memory%20and%20History.pdf.

Schleser, M., Wilson, G., & Keep, D. (2013, October). Small screen and big screen: Mobile film-making in Australasia, ubiquity. *The Journal of Pervasive Media, 2*(1–2), 118–131.

Van Dijck, J. (2007). *Mediated memories in the digital age*. Stanford, CA: Stanford University Press.

Wood, A. (2007). *Digital encounters*. London: Routledge.

CHAPTER 6

Wayfaring, Creating and Performing with Smartphones

Jess Kilby and Marsha Berry

Abstract The development of camera phones in the mid-2000s has generated new ways of making mobile art. Wayfaring, co-presence and mobility are concepts through which mobile media art can be reimagined. Our ability to easily document our movements through everyday life has shifted how we think about film and photography. This is the background for the creative practice research discussed here. This chapter asks: "What new forms of creative expressions are emerging and in what ways is creative practice research engaging with them?" The authors cast themselves as digital wayfarers whose online and physical worlds are entangled in urban and coastal places to research some of the creative possibilities to photographers, artists and writers presented by the extreme accessibility of smartphones. In this chapter, the focus is on the making of creative works.

Keywords Digital wayfaring · Place · Smartphone

J. Kilby (✉) · M. Berry
RMIT University, Melbourne, Australia

© The Author(s) 2018
M. Schleser and M. Berry (eds.), *Mobile Story Making in an Age of Smartphones*, https://doi.org/10.1007/978-3-319-76795-6_6

We begin this chapter with a question that goes to the heart of creative practice-based research. What new forms of creative expressions are emerging, and in what ways is creative practice research engaging with them? We follow Haseman's (2006) definition of practice-based research as "concerned with the improvement of practice, and new epistemologies of practice distilled from the insider's understandings of action in context" (Haseman 2006, p. 100). Walking with smartphones is a method integral to each of our respective art practices. As we walk, we write on our smartphones as well as take photographs and video.

Our Inspiration

In previous work, Berry (2008) observed that locative media art has some resonances with the Situationist movement of the 1960s where artists intervened in the urban landscape to provide alternate visions and readings of urban spaces. Where the Situationists used physical space, locative media artists also use telecommunications networks to create contemporary commentaries of urban spaces. The spirit of the Situationist movement has been reincarnated in much recent locative media art. Even though our method is walking, we diverge from psychogeography and the Situationists in that we do not set ourselves the rules and constraints that are hallmarks of this genre of locative media art. We unfold our methods and creative practices in the next section.

Being and walking in landscapes has an interior as well as an exterior dynamic so that a "landscape is situated in the expression and poetics of spacing: apprehended as constituted in a flirtatious mode: contingent, sensual, anxious, awkward" (Crouch 2010, p. 7). In short, it is an experience that is mutable, complex and intangible, and it can inspire the making of creative responses (Heidegger 1996). In the second decade of the twenty-first-century, being and walking in landscapes also has a networked dimension because of smartphone assemblages.

Here, we present some of our mobile media art experiments engaging with the extreme accessibility of smartphone cameras. Through examples drawn from our collective creative practices, we unfold evidence showing how mobile media and the extreme accessibility of the means of production moves filmmaking and mobile media art into new forms. Non-representational theoretical concepts (Ingold 2010, 2015) provide a way for us to situate the dynamic and intricate relations between creative practices with smartphones and everyday life. In a nutshell, non-representational theory is concerned with the ever-changing liveliness, mutability and dynamism of the routine practices and activities of everyday life rather than the symbolic and representational dimensions. This chapter captures some of the more-than-representational, the more-than-textual multisensory aspects of our respective creative practice research with smartphone cameras to contribute to current and ongoing debates about how mobile media is transforming our social and creative practices.

What our methodologies have in common is an approach informed by non-representational theory, as put forward by anthropologist Tim Ingold. To use Ingold's words, we look for moments where correspondence arises between "things and happenings going on around us" and for the opportunity "of answering to them with interventions, questions, and responses of our own" (Ingold 2015, p. vii). We construct landscapes through our walking, inscribing ourselves into landscapes so that

> Landscape as practice or art practice is forwarded into process, as dynamic rather than either 'outside' experience or only focused through the physical character of encounters. (Crouch 2010, p. 14)

We explore two quite different types of places—urban laneways and coastal paths—through our practice-based mobile art research. The paths we wend through physical environments are paramount to the mobile art projects we present here. To help explain our methods involving wayfaring and wayfinding further, we turn to the work of Argounova-Low (2012). In her study of walking as a method to understand places and their narratives, she invoked the concept word hodology. Hodology as used by Argounova-Low (2012) refers to the study of paths and has its origins in Greek (*hodos* meaning way, road, journey) and provides a way to conceive of place as dynamic, constantly changing and subject to the forces of the weather. Argounova-Low suggests that "the hodological approach underlines the very flow of both roads and narratives" (2012, p. 195). We both use a hodological approach (see Argounova-Low 2012) to explore connections and flows between poetic expressions, places and landscapes, for, as Lee and Ingold argue, "walking allows for an understanding of places being created by routes" (2006, p. 68). We cast ourselves as digital wayfarers following Hjorth and Pink (2014):

> the digital wayfarer as we conceptualize her or him does not simply weave her or his way around the material physical world. Rather, their trajectory

entangles online and offline as they move through the weather and the air, with the ground underfoot and surrounded by people and things, while also traversing digital maps, social networking sites, and other online elements. (Hjorth and Pink 2014, pp. 45–46)

In the following section we present an unconventional braided account of our respective practices using vignettes describing our practice and process. There are interleaved with scholarly literature to situate our practice within broader theoretical and cultural frames. For this reason, in the next section we use the singular first person to provide an insider's perspective of how the "I" uses smartphones to create mobile art.

Vignettes of Digital Wayfaring

The notion of wayfaring, or travelling by foot, has always evoked a corollary of wayfinding—of navigating the traversal of a space. This need not necessarily be *toward* a finite destination—indeed, wayfaring implies a delicious lack of such rational design—but rather *through* a territory that has dimensions both external and internal. This wayfinding applies equally to familiar, unfamiliar and once-familiar terrain, each kind of journey tending to tap into different frequencies of place.

In the spirit of both wayfaring and wayfinding, we offer a series of vignettes drawn from our respective practices with our smartphones that themselves traverse a space: the space of a digital wayfaring art practice finding its way into being. Kilby traverses urban laneways; Berry walks along coastal paths.

1—Kilby

I have always been a wanderer of neighbourhoods. When I was 13 years old this wandering led me to discover a place called Hidden City, secreted away in the forests of my hometown. It was a discovery that forever changed my perception of the everyday.

Riding my bike toward the outskirts of town one summer afternoon, I noticed a dirt track leading off from the main road into the dense woods beyond, so I did what any 13-year-old with a brand-new mountain bike would do: I steered into the trees. As I pedalled deeper into the forest, there came the glint of something strange: a chrome bumper. Then, a bedroom window. Cars. Houses. Laughter, somewhere. The wafting scent of barbeque.

I knew these woods. And yet here was a mysterious enclave that I had somehow missed, less than a mile from my own house. An entire neighbourhood, fifty acres large, accessible by nothing more than a dirt track. I felt like I had stumbled into another world.

2—Kilby

Adulthood took me to new neighbourhoods, where I would write new fables. Love, loss, longing, uncertainty—a life no more or less extraordinary than the next. And for a long time I forgot about those houses in the woods. But eventually I found myself grappling with a story that seemed impossible to write. It was too big, too painful, too much of a conclusion despite the new beginning that it implied. In search of something that I could not name, I found my way back out into the neighbourhood. For hours and hours, I would walk. As I settled into the solace of this routine, strange things began to catch my eye. Messages, they almost seemed. Because I had my phone with me, I started photographing them. And while my painful story still needed to be written, these walks enlarged from solace into something larger and more luminous.

3—Kilby

A decade later, a Ph.D. My proposal: to make a game about discovering secret cities hiding in plain sight. I started with my sketchbook; with plans, ideas. I struggled to bring these ideas to life. Each design seemed too detailed and yet too hollow to create the kind of experience that I was after: an encounter with the wonder of the everyday.

After several false starts I surrendered for a while. Summer had quietly become autumn; I was ending a relationship. I had signed a six-month lease on a doomed old house in an unfamiliar suburb and I had done all of the unpacking that I planned to do. I started walking, and I took my phone with me.

My new suburb squatted indifferently on the border between urban and suburban Melbourne, dropping off at one edge into a deep valley. The place was a void; a blank spot in my mind. My house sat at the bottom of the valley and the nothingness seemed to gather there. The only time I felt the world come back to me was when I escaped on to the endless concrete ribbon of the Capital City Trail, following the winding path up over the freeway and down under it again, along the squalid creek that had been concreted in so heavily that I first mistook it for a drain.

I was haunting the ragged edge of the city, and although I didn't fully realise it, I was lonely. The images I brought back from those walks were postcards, messages from absent others. I made my own memories out of what they left behind: graffiti, a loaf of bread, a tattered armchair with a view. One day I came across two shopping trolleys tipped sideways in the middle of the creek. They looked almost sculptural, and at the same time morosely out of place. I photographed them. Over the next few months I began to encounter more abandoned trolleys in strange places. They were in pairs, gangs, never alone. I photographed them too. The day before I moved out, coming down a long, steep set of stairs in a park just by my house, I met a lone trolley leaning crookedly against the rail. A front wheel dangled freely.

"Go home, trolley. You're drunk," I muttered fondly, and took one last photo before I left.

4—Kilby

When my lease was up I moved out of death valley and into a new neighbourhood, where I finally tried to bring my game into the world. It was only a fragment of a game; I didn't know where it might lead—if anywhere at all—but this seemed to be the only way to start.

The first evening of the game I went out wandering my neighbourhood, looking for semi-secret spots to leave small tokens that were meant to be an invitation into the game. Again I brought my phone, but mostly to document the leaving of the tokens (Fig. 6.1).

Random encounters in public spaces underpin the concept of psychogeography as theorised by Ivan Chtcheglov (1953). Psychogeography is a way of knowing the urbanscape through experience, for instance, walking. Whilst walking, a person may have a chance encounter with something surprising. Such encounters are a common trope in many recent locative media works. McCullough (2006) argues that the application of locative media can contribute to enhance the richness of the city and identifies "urban markup" as something that can "attach as new layers to the forms and flows of the city". Urban markup is also a theme taken up by Farman, who notes that it "can be done through durable inscription (like words carved into a durable façade of a building or statue) or through ephemeral inscriptions (ranging from banners and billboards to graffiti and stickers)" (Farman 2014, p. 4).

Fig. 6.1 Image of a token in situ. ©Jess Kilby, 2014

But neither Kilby's nor Berry's inspiration came from psychogeography or from the Situationists. To explore this divergence further, we present an additional vignette derived from Kilby's process.

5—Kilby

As I continued to explore my neighbourhood, with the tokens and then more so with my phone camera, I became increasingly aware that in fact I was the player of this game. Or, at least, that I was one of the players. And perhaps—although maybe this is hindsight—that the making of the game was actually the game?

In the beginning, this had been about the tokens: about leaving them, about them being taken. But in the end the tokens turned out to be merely a device for tuning in to something more. The real game was between the streets and me—and the camera seemed to be my constant intermediary (Fig. 6.2).

Psychogeography as posited by Debord is concerned with constraints and rules. Kilby deliberately resisted and broke her desire to impose rules and constraints. Her interventions have strong resonances with the French artist Le Goff as described by cultural geographer Jill Fenton:

> Invariably, Le Goff's interventions encompass the discovery and leaving of objects as signs in their own right, and these become traces of what has taken place. Frequently, because they are subjected to the elements or are taken as found objects by passers-by or collectors, such objects have a transient life. (Fenton 2005, p. 423)

Fig. 6.2   Tokens speak back, smartphone photograph. ©Jess Kilby, 2015

Such traces are also present in Berry's practice. However, in Berry's case, digital co-presence grounds her mobile art, as evident in the vignette below, which provides an analytical yet evocative description of her process.

6—Berry

The coastal path winds over the top of the bluff through indigenous flora including banksias and sheoaks. The sky is bright blue, the shadows sharp. The sea is choppy. I tread lightly, so many footprints—human and animal—piping seagulls, a counterpoint to the restless sea. A perfect moment—I post photos of various details of sandy path on Instagram and Facebook with short evocative captions. A left-behind skirt flaps helplessly on the fence bordering the path.

I continued to shoot video with my smartphone while walking. I worked intuitively, intentionally, without any specific intention other than simply to notice as much as possible whilst walking along a coastal trail.

The comments on my Facebook post show me that people are with me; we are walking together, experiencing the coastal path. I notice that my interlocutors are pulling my images into a virtual trail of their own, but theirs is a narrative, a guided tour rather than a sequence of moments in the lifeworld of a coastal path. The seed for a film is sown—a female voice-over, poetic meanderings and double exposures (Fig. 6.3).

Non-representational theory as understood by Ingold provided Berry with a frame within which to situate her practice. In "Footprints through the weather-world: Walking, breathing knowing" (2010), Ingold explored the relations between walking, the weather, and knowing or being knowledgeable. He argued that

> Breathing with every step they take, wayfarers walk at once in the air and on the ground. This walking is itself a process of thinking and knowing. Thus knowledge is formed along paths of movement in the weather-world. (Ingold 2010, S121)

Ingold's (2010) statement that wayfarers walk in the air as well as on the ground reminded Berry that the air is not only subject to the forces of the weather, but is also a space of telecommunications signals, or, to put

Fig. 6.3   Screenshot from *Wayfarer's Trail*, a smartphone film. ©Marsha Berry, 2016

it another way, the air is host to Hertzian space (Dunne 2001). A digital wayfarer with a smartphone walks not only in what Ingold conceptualises as the weather-world, but also traverses Hertzian space.

CONCLUSION

Our ability to document our movements through everyday life has shifted how we think about film and photography. Mobile media has disrupted traditional media distribution power relationships to open up new expressive potentials as we collectively grapple with the everyday realities of networked co-presence, virtual proximity, and what these can mean for our everyday social activities and rituals. Through our practice-based research motivated by our research question about screen production we have found that we have all become digital wayfarers each in our own way—the phone camera serving as compass as we navigate and create the landscapes of our daily lives—and that this has opened new terrains for mobile art as well as new forms of screen production.

BIBLIOGRAPHY

Argounova-Low, T. (2012). Narrating the road. *Landscape Research, 37*(2), 191–206.

Bauman, Z. (2003). *Liquid love: On the frailty of human bonds.* Cambridge: Polity Press.

Berry, M. (2008). Locative media: Geoplaced tactics of resistance. *International Journal of Performing Arts and Digital Media, 4*(2–3), 101–116. (Intellect, Great Britain).

Chtcheglov, I. (1953). *Formulary for a new urbanism.* Summary/Notes. http://witold.postagon.com/91myy64da [accessed 17 June 2017].

Crouch, D. (2010). Flirting with space: Thinking landscape relationally. *Cultural Geographies, 17*(1), 5–18.

Dunne, A. (2001). *Hertzian tales: Electronic products, aesthetic experience, and critical design.* Cambridge, MA: MIT Press.

Farman, J. (2014). *The mobile story: Narrative practices with locative technologies.* London: Routledge.

Fenton, J. (2005). Space, chance, time: Walking backwards through the hours on the left and right banks of Paris. *Cultural Geographies, 12*(4), 412–428.

Haseman, B. C. (2006). A manifesto for performative research. *Media International Australia Incorporating Culture and Policy: Quarterly Journal of Media Research and Resources, 118*, 98–106.

Heidegger, M. (1996). *Being and time.* Albany: State University of New York Press.

Hjorth, L., & Pink, S. (2014). New visualities and the digital wayfarer: Reconceptualizing camera phone photography and locative media. *Mobile Media & Communication, 2*(1), 40–57.

Ingold, T. (2010). Footprints through the weather-world: Walking, breathing, knowing. *Journal of the Royal Anthropological Institute (N.S.), 16*, S121–S139.

Ingold, T. (2015). Foreword. In P. Vannini (Ed.), *Non-representational methodologies: Re-envisioning research* (pp. vii–viii). New York & London: Routledge.

Lee, J., & Ingold, T. (2006). Fieldwork on foot: Perceiving, routing, socializing. In S. Coleman & P. Collins (Eds.), *Locating the field: Space, place and context in anthropology.* Oxford: Berg.

McCullough. (2006). On urban markup: Frames of reference in location models for participatory urbanism. *Leonardo Online.* http://leoalmanac.org/journal/vol_14/lea_v14_n03-04/mmccullough.asp [accessed 16 June 2017].

PART II

Making Spaces

CHAPTER 7

Perspectives on Music Sharing via Mobile Phones in Papua New Guinea

Oli Wilson

Abstract The research presented in this chapter seeks to broaden our understanding and perception of the contemporary media landscape by examining the application of new digital communication technologies in Papua New Guinea (PNG). Mobile phones have recently become widespread in certain areas of PNG, a country renowned in the western popular imagination for its remoteness and ancient traditions. PNG also hosts a vibrant popular music culture, which is due in part to the increased global availability of digital recording technologies. This chapter explores how the contemporary consumption of popular music via mobile phones reflects local social and cultural practices relating to the Melanesian gift-economy, while demonstrating new adaptations and sharing practices among diverse urban youth.

Keywords Music sharing · Mobile apps

O. Wilson (✉)
Massey University, Wellington, New Zealand

© The Author(s) 2018
M. Schleser and M. Berry (eds.), *Mobile Story Making in an Age of Smartphones*, https://doi.org/10.1007/978-3-319-76795-6_7

65

This chapter explores mobile phone-oriented music sharing practices among groups of university students in the town of Madang in Papua New Guinea (PNG). In other publications, I have described local popular music as a distinctively indigenous mode of creative expression that mobilises global music formats in accordance with local socialities (Wilson 2011, 2013, 2014a, b). This chapter demonstrates how contemporary consumption of popular music via mobile phones also reflects music's capacity to foster social connectivity through sharing, while also acting as a marker of exclusion and social status. In PNG, digital music sharing is usually done in person, and this aspect reflects unique cultural practices not usually associated with mobile phones. Much of the music being shared in PNG contains little information or metadata discernible to those outside of small family-oriented social networks, and therefore "it is the practices surrounding the objects that represent the music that we must turn to" (Crowdy 2015, p. 67). In this chapter, I demonstrate that in PNG the interpersonal nature of file sharing distinguishes it from the practice of online file sharing as a form of music consumption, as understood in western contexts (see Huang 2005, for example). The resulting sharing practices reflect emerging yet distinctively indigenous values about sharing, which can be viewed in the context of the Melanesian gift-economy and are evident through the socio-cultural politics that surround music sharing.

Mobile Phone Technology in PNG

Mobile phone use in PNG has grown significantly since 2007, and much of this growth has occurred in rural areas. This has been largely attributed to the expansion of the telecommunications company Digicel due to market deregulation. Prior to Digicel's involvement in PNG, mobile coverage was limited to urban centres, and was available exclusively through the state-owned Telikom PNG (see Suwamaru 2015; Suwamaru and Anderson 2012). By 2014, following the expansion of Digicel phone towers throughout rural areas, approximately 41% of the population was estimated to have regular access to a mobile phone.[1] It is believed that by the end of 2008 subscription to mobile services in PNG had reached 1 million connections, mostly on the Digicel service (Bruett and Firpo 2009). Accordingly, a handful of studies have investigated the local impact that this new technology, or, as one researcher labelled it, the "new communication drum of Papua New Guinea" (Watson 2011), is having among rural communities (Telban and Vávrová 2014).

MOBILE PHONES AND MUSIC SHARING

In the following analysis, I point to a number of key capacities about popular music and sharing that I have observed, namely: the capacity for music to strengthen social relationships among relatives and members of one's own cultural group; the capacity for music sharing to foster social relationships among students from culturally diverse backgrounds; the capacity for music to act as a conduit for linguistic sharing (which also serves to initiate and strengthen social relationships among students from diverse backgrounds); and, lastly, the capacity of music to act as a marker and enforcer of social status among young people through acts of sharing as well as the act of not sharing.

My first point concerns attitudes relating to sharing among relatives. This process is particularly pertinent when considering the indigenous system of exchange and reciprocity called the *wantok* system, which connects individuals through a marriage and kinship-based system of exchange and reciprocity (see Goddard 2005, p. 13; Sillitoe 2000, p. 169).[2] The system functions as a kind of social security, as there is no state-funded welfare system. Individuals are obliged to provide for relatives depending on their birth or marriage-defined relationship.

The gift economy in Melanesia has been explored in considerable detail in a number of seminal anthropological studies (Gregory 1980; Malinowski 2002; Strathern 1988). These assert that gift and exchange systems are central to the social and political organisation of Melanesian societies. From the perspective of the participants in this research, the notion of giving and reciprocating forms a fundamental part of how many Papua New Guineans identify their own culture.

> We give and take. Sometimes you might be in need. So when people ask you to share things, they'll know that it's like, necessary. We have this payback system where you give and then when you are in need, then someone's going to give you something or they will help you. When you share things, then you become better friends with people, [because] they know that you share things. (Participant in group 2, 22 September 2015)

Sharing among family is a common practice. An important factor in sharing among family members is the type of music being shared. Students reported sharing music with relatives from the region that they identified with as a means to strengthen their connections to that place and those relatives. This is particularly pertinent when considering that urban centres in PNG are relatively new, and that many of those who reside there maintain strong connections to rural places that they identify as "home" (see Sillitoe 2000, p. 164). One student who identified as being from the city of Rabaul explained: "When I listen to songs [from Rabaul], and I'm far away from home, it brings my mind back to where I come from" (Participant in group 2, 29 September 2015). Even students who were born in Port Moresby—a city, and thus not normally associated with rural place signifiers—reported a strong relationship with songs sung in the indigenous language of their parents', or grandparents', "home". A student remarked:

> Because I grew up in Port Moresby, I lived there my whole life, but when I listen to [songs from Rabaul] it reminds me of home [...] of my childhood and my uncles and my dad, everyone sitting around. (Participant in group 4, 29 September 2015)

Students reported that sharing music is also an important way to get to know each other:

> Most of the people we share music with have become good friends with us by just sharing music. (Participant in group 2, 29 September 2015)

It is here that new sharing practices are observed and relate to both locally produced and international music. When someone shares a song with another individual, the giver becomes connected to that particular song. One student noted that when someone plays or shares a song:

> People know who gave that person the song [...] we feel [connected] in a way, like we're the owner of the song. (Participant in group 2, 22 September 2015)

The culturally diverse student body at DWU provides the backdrop for cross-cultural music sharing. Students viewed this diversity as positive and emphasised music's role in building social connections among individuals who identify with different cultural groups:

We try to mix around and get to know each other. One way is by listening to their songs, and then if I listen to her songs, she's from the Highlands and I'm from the Island areas [...] I get her songs and I can ask her to translate what does this song mean, and she will translate. Then I get a fair idea of what her culture is like, and what her language is like. (Participant in group 2, 22 September 2015)

Learning each other's culture and language is an important social activity among friends from diverse groups:

All of us are looking for the meaning of the lyrics, and they are looking for the meaning. So they might ask us "what's the meaning of this word?" and we will translate it. (Participant in group 2, 22 September 2015)

In some cases, however, participants reported not wanting to share songs. The most common scenario concerned newly released songs. When a student was the only person in a friend group with a particular new song, he or she may be initially reluctant to share. One student explained:

When I listen to a certain song and people pass by or my friends, and they say "oh, I like that song we want to have it" then I usually share it with them, [but] sometimes when I download new songs, I really don't share it because I just want to listen to it and I want to be the first person to know the lyrics and everything first. Once it gets popular and everybody is listening to it, then I will share it. Otherwise I'll say, "go look for your own!" (Participant "Granger", 26 September 2015)

While this seems in contradiction to the previous affirmative notions of sharing, new songs are treated differently because of the capital they represent. Although the students have not purchased the song from an aggregator or distribution service, they have purchased the data, and therefore are perceived to have some kind of ownership rights over that song until it enters the public domain. A student explained:

I will pay for the data to go online and download this song. So I want to have it to myself. I'm greedy sometimes with the songs [because] I spend the money to get it, then I have the right to hold on to it for longer. (Participant in group 4, 29 September 2015)

However, within a week or so the song becomes public either via the radio, or through others also downloading it, and is then likely to be shared more freely. The song's capacity to reflect capital is therefore temporary and tied to its scarcity. Further, students who have access to more financial support and, in turn, more data are in a position to exercise their economic status through strategic sharing practices. Scarcity of songs is also significantly enhanced when the song in question is evidently popular, or by an already popular artist.

Despite this, students almost unanimously reported sharing new popular songs with their closest friends and family members. When individuals bypassed their closest and established network and received songs from another source, this was sometimes seen as a kind of social taboo. There was also some indication that students born in Port Moresby were less inclined to share freely, and more inclined to establish their social status through music non-sharing, as one student explained:

> I have a few friends in Port Moresby, they always like to play the latest music and they don't share until it gets really old [...] I think they think it makes them cooler if they have new songs and nobody else has them. (Participant in group 4, 29 September 2015)

Students did not seem overly concerned about being denied songs, especially from those with whom they do not have strong relationships. One student suggested:

> I take no for an answer, and I don't think it's a big deal. Many times people tend to say "no [you can't have a copy of this song]", so it's normal, [especially] if it's a new song. (Participant in group 4, 29 September 2015)

CONCLUSIONS

Sharing culture is an important part of PNG identity and music sharing reflects a new way of defining contemporary social relations. This research provides further evidence that new technologies are not having a homogenisation effect on local cultures.[3] Rather, it reveals considerable variation across globally diverse cultures and positions media and media technologies as simultaneously material and embedded within social practices. The cultural politics surrounding music sharing via smartphones points to "the ways in which cultures embed technologies"

(Ihde 1990, p. 124, italics in original), meaning that the broader local cultural frameworks must be foregrounded in order to understand how new technologies are impacting local cultures, and how local cultures are defining the way new technologies are adopted. In PNG, this has been observed in mobile phone use among the Karawari people in the East Sepik Province. Here, mobile phone use is "framed by cosmologically well-established desires to deepen the contacts with the usually invisible (external) world [...] and bring all the advantages available to [deceased relatives] into their living presence" (Telban and Vávrová 2014, p. 224).

In this study, sharing is understood to be part of what makes PNG unique as a collection of cultures. In this sense, desires for new technologies in PNG should be understood to be historically constituted, and do not indicate that technologies automatically drive a shift away from traditional values towards modern ones. However, this position does not unanimously reflect localised narratives surrounding new technologies, and in particular music, which has been surrounded by fears of "cultural grey-out" (Philpott 1995). In general, students felt that mobile phones had a positive impact on their life and culture, though other studies have shown this not to be universal (for example Watson 2011).

The processes and social contexts I have explored above can be further understood by considering them in relation to observations made by Monica Stern, who observes that popular music in Vanuatu is not merely a leisure activity, but a constituent part of social relations (Stern 2014). The sharing practices observed in my research also indicate the importance of music in establishing social relationships, but also the direction of power dynamics between youth with access to music-sharing technologies. Here, sharing is positioned within the context of gift relationships, and in the PNG context reflects unique cultural practices not normally associated with mobile phones. The key capacities that I observed throughout this chapter reflect distinctively indigenous values about sharing and are evident through socio-cultural politics around sharing. These point to new ways that the actions of sharing, or not sharing, are being mobilised among young people as a social enabler in a multicultural urban context through which language and kin-based social structures are being redefined.

NOTES

1. See http://www.worldbank.org/en/news/feature/2015/09/29/connecting-the-unconnected-in-papua-new-guinea.
2. *Wantok* translates as 'one talk' in English and refers to a member of the same language group.
3. Like globalised cultural, economic, and migratory 'scapes' (Appadurai 1996).

BIBLIOGRAPHY

Andersen, B. (2013). Tricks, lies, and mobile phones: 'Phone Friend' stories in Papua New Guinea. *Culture, Theory and Critique, 54*(1), 318–334.

Appadurai, A. (1996). *Modernity at large: Cultural dimensions of globalization.* Minneapolis, MN: University of Minnesota Press.

Bruett, T., & Firpo, J. (2009). *Building a mobile money distribution network in Papua New Guinea.* Retrieved from http://www.uncdf.org/en/node/2296.

Crowdy, D. (2015). When digital is physical and ethnomusicologists are file sharers. *Journal of World Popular Music, 2*(1), 61–77.

Goddard, M. (2005). *The unseen city: Anthropological perspectives on Port Moresby, Papua New Guinea.* Canberra: Pandanus Books.

Gregory, C. A. (1980). Gifts to men and gifts to God: Gift exchange and capital accumulation in contemporary Papua. *Man, 15*(4), 626–652.

Huang, C. (2005). File sharing as a form of music consumption. *International Journal of Electronic Commerce, 9*(4), 37–55.

Ihde, D. (1990). *Technology and the lifeworld: From garden to earth* (No. 560). Bloomington: Indiana University Press.

Kaleebu, N., Gee, A., Maybanks, N., Jones, R., Jauk, M., & Watson, A. H. (2014). SMS story: Early results of an innovative education trial. *Contemporary PNG Studies, 19,* 50.

Lipset, D. (2013). Mobail: Moral ambivalence and the domestication of mobile telephones in peri-urban Papua New Guinea. *Culture, Theory and Critique, 54*(3), 335–354.

Malinowski, B. (2002). *Argonauts of the Western Pacific: An account of native enterprise and adventure in the archipelagoes of Melanesian New Guinea.* London: Routledge (reprint).

Philpott, M. (1995). Developments in Papua New Guinea's popular music industry: The media and technological change in a country with many cultures. *Perfect Beat, 2*(3), 98–114.

Sillitoe, P. (2000). *Social change in Melanesia: Development and history.* Cambridge: Cambridge University Press.

Stern, M. (2014). "Mi wantem musik blong mi hemi blong evriwan" ["I want my music to be for everyone"]: Digital developments, copyright and music circulation in Port Vila, Vanuatu. *First Monday, 19*(10), Retrieved from http://firstmonday.org/ojs/index.php/fm/article/view/5551.

Strathern, M. (1988). *The gender of the gift: Problems with women and problems with society in Melanesia* (Vol. 6). Berkeley: University of California Press.

Suwamaru, J. K. (2015). Aspects of mobile phone usage in Papua New Guinea: A socio-economic perspective. *Contemporary PNG Studies: DWU Research Journal, 22,* 1–16.

Suwamaru, J. K., & Anderson, P. K. (2012). Closing the digital divide in Papua New Guinea: A proposal for a national telecommunications model. *Contemporary PNG Studies, 17*(1), 1–15.

Telban, B., & Vávrová, D. (2014). Ringing the living and the dead: Mobile phones in a Sepik society. *Australian Journal of Anthropology, 25*(2), 223–238. https://doi.org/10.1111/taja.12090.

United Nations Development Programme. (2014). *2014 National Human Development Report: Papua New Guinea.* Retrieved from http://hdr.undp.org/en/content/papua-new-guinea-national-human-development-report-2014.

van der Vlies, M., & Watson, A. H. (2014). *Can mobile phones help reduce teacher absenteeism in Papua New Guinea.* Paper submitted for publication in the proceedings of the Australian and New Zealand Communication Association Annual Conference, Swinburne University, Victoria.

Watson, A. H. (2011). *The mobile phone: The new communication drum of Papua New Guinea.* Doctoral dissertation, Queensland University of Technology.

Watson, A. H. (2014, June 12–13). *Facilitating economic development through the use of mobile phones.* Unpublished paper presented at PNG Update at the Unviersity of Papua New Guinea.

Wilson, O. (2011). Papua New Guinea: Popular music and the continuity of tradition—An ethnography of songs from the band Paramana Strangers. In G. Baldacchino (Ed.), *Island songs: A global repertoire* (pp. 119–135). Plymouth: Scarecrow Press.

Wilson, O. (2013). Popular music as local culture: An ethnographic study of the Album Matha Wa! by the Band Paramana Strangers from Papua New Guinea. *Musicology Australia, 35*(2), 253–267.

Wilson, O. (2014a). Ples and popular music production: A typology of home-based recording studios in Port Moresby, Papua New Guinea. *Ethnomusicology Forum, 23*(3), 425–444.

Wilson, O. (2014b). Selling lokal music: A comparison of the content and promotion of two locally recorded and released albums in Port Moresby, Papua New Guinea. *World of Popular Music, 1*(1), 51–72.

CHAPTER 8

Stories from the Field: Playing with Mobile Media

Larissa Hjorth and Ingrid Richardson

Abstract Mobile media has become a crucial part of everyday storytelling. As we move through our daily rhythms and rituals, mobile media weave multiple cartographies—visual, social, spatial and temporal. Far from placeless, the history of mobile media has been one in which the important stories of place and locality are reinforced. By contextualising story-making through early explorations into mobile media as art and alternative modes of learning, Hjorth and Richardson reflect upon how play can provide a productive lens for understanding mobile storytelling. They then explore a series of play workshops that were founded to think through the role of mobile games in everyday life and as part of place-making techniques.

Keywords Mobile games · Mobile media · Locative media

L. Hjorth (✉)
RMIT University, Melbourne, VIC, Australia

I. Richardson
Murdoch University, Perth, WA, Australia

© The Author(s) 2018   75
M. Schleser and M. Berry (eds.), *Mobile Story Making in an Age of Smartphones*, https://doi.org/10.1007/978-3-319-76795-6_8

Mobile media has become a crucial part of everyday storytelling. As we move through our daily rhythms and rituals, mobile media weave multiple cartographies—visual, social, spatial and temporal. In these movements, the online and offline entangle in different ways that can be characterised as playful (Sicart 2014) and representative of the ongoing ludification of culture (Frissen et al. 2015).

Far from placeless, the history of mobile media has been one in which the importance of place and locality is reinforced (Ito 2003; Ozkul 2014; Pink and Hjorth 2012). Through the lens of mobile media, we can begin to complicate the ways in which place and co-presence are conceptualised and practised. If, as Massey identified, space is "a simultaneity of stories-so-far" and "places are collections of those stories" (Massey 2005, p. 130), then mobile media—as a probe, tool, content and vehicle—plays a key role in both the collecting and contextualisation of ethnographic data. Mobile media shifts between being the researcher's and participant)'s tool, medium and subject matter.

The rising significance of playful mobile media within quotidian life can be paralleled to shifts in definitions of cartography in what has been called the "critical cartography" turn (Wilmott 2013). For Chris Perkins (2012), maps and mapping practices have become integral to our everyday place-making (Verhoeff 2012) and can be understood as part of a broader ludic shift whereby playing no longer happens *on* maps but *in* maps. Drawing on Raessen's (2006) discussion of the ludification of culture, whereby play increasingly performs a key role in everyday life, Perkins argues that cartography is now informed by location-based mobile gaming and the ways in which playful collaboration can lead to new ways of "telling" and visualising place. As Perkins notes, applications such as desktop mapping and geographic information systems (GIS) have democratised the tools for cartography and in turn made mapping "no longer tied to fixed specifications" (2012, p. 2). In this shift, playful mobile media figures predominantly, and we must now understand contesting places and spaces though a variety of cartographic practices (technological, social, electronic, emotional, geographic to name a few).

Through the trope of the playful, innovative methods and approaches with and towards media emerge (Hjorth et al. 2016). Playful use of mobile media has a long interdisciplinary tradition (Hjorth and Richardson 2014; de Souza e Silva and Hjorth 2009). In both innovative art and ethnographic research, bringing play to a notion of knowledge transmission is important, as play can take multiple roles such as cultural probe, mode of inquiry and context (Hjorth and Byrne 2016).

In this chapter, we think through the role of mobile media as a site for the coalescence of digital and non-digital story-making. By contextualising story-making through early explorations into mobile media as art and alternative modes of learning we reflect upon how play can provide a productive lens for understanding mobile storytelling.

THE MOBILE FIELD: MOBILE LEARNING AND REFLECTIVE CREATIVE PRACTICE IN THE FIELD

In the space of mobile learning, locations such as Japan have been seminal. In particular, the works of Fumitoshi Kato (2014) and Shin Mizukoshi (2003) have sought to define the important role of mobile media as tools for creative practice and community participatory design. For fifteen years, Kato's work with Japanese students using mobile weblogs (moblogs) for creative reflective practice with communities has undergone many iterations as mobile technology advances. Kato's action research has in various ways sought to explore the mobile phone as a vehicle, tool and mode of practice in fieldwork, especially through camera phone online archiving and sharing via moblogs. When Kato began his moblog work around 2000, Japan was one of the few countries with camera phones. In 1999, Japanese company Kyocera launched the first inbuilt camera "Visual Phone" which, in turn, established Japan as a pioneer in the growth of mobile visuality. Camera phone images have played a dual role as both a mode of intimate sharing and as a way of providing users with the ability to create personal archives as an extended form of diarisation (Kato 2014).

Mizukoshi's (2003) participatory design work also sought to think about mobile media as contributing to new forms of literacy. Unlike Kato's work, which focused upon mobile visuality, Mizukoshi explored the multimodal dimensions of literacy. Mizukoshi's work can be seen as an early model of the "living lab" idea in which everyday life contexts become the site for ethnographic exploration. While Mizukoshi's work created incubators in the classroom for students to experiment around mobile media, Kato's work focused upon students in the fieldsite of the community whereby researchers and participants would work collaboratively with community members and then share particular meaningful stories about and with the community. In the early days, the quality of the mobile phone images were poor and mocking up videos and posters took much time and equipment. Today, students can bring their smartphones (*sumaho*) into the field as a tool for data collection, reflection and creative practice outputs. In these fieldsites, the lines between the *sumaho* as field-work collector and curator blur in interesting ways to reveal how community stories are made at the juncture of online networks and place.

The early pioneering work of Kato and Mizukoshi presciently explored some of the key and multiple roles played by mobile media in the field and in the creation and collection of data. Mobile media are intrinsically bound to both the co-present and co-located role of the researcher in online and offline contexts. As tools of and for intimate exchange, mobile media as the researcher's tool reveals particular relationships between intimacy and disclosure. The act of recording via the phone—as a mundane and familiar device—is much less invasive than a professional or dedicated camera. Mobile media create a particular entanglement between co-presence and co-location for the researcher and the field highlighting Anne Beaulieu's argument that ethnographers need to rethink not only of the politics and practice of co-presence but also of co-location (2010).

As Martin Rieser (2011) notes in *The mobile audiences: Media art and mobile technologies*, mobile technologies are affording new types of audience engagement, art and narrative forms. In particular, as discussed by Adriana de Souza e Silva in "Art by telephone: From static to mobile interfaces" (2004), locative art projects have historically been synonymous with early mobile art through collectives like Blast Theory. These projects overtly engaged with the changing fabric of urbanity and how we in turn reconceptualise space and storify place. However, just as smartphones blur social, locative and mobile media across a variety of contexts, modes of presence and media, mobile art has become increasingly diverse and ambiguous, especially in terms of blurring new media and art. Mobile art is as contested as it is divergent, representing a challenge to what constitutes art and the mobile.

For Mimi Sheller (2014), mobile art is characterised by *mediality*—that is, a reflexive form of enacted and mediated spatiality. Sheller's examples focus predominantly upon media art case studies that overtly engage with the entanglement between network and place. What becomes apparent is mobile media are no longer devices just for "new media" artists. Rather, they are providing new canvases, multimedia tools, contexts and social worlds for artists to enact playful interventions. This is highlighted by Mann Bartlett's work in which he toys with mobile media as a medium for the social. As Hjorth, King and Kataoka note, as mobile media render the intimate *public* and the public *intimate*, the roles of place, art practice and politics are transformed, which in turn provide new models for engagement, distribution and participation (2014).

Mobile art is no longer just a site for artist dissemination or self-promotion via social media, but an active part of everyday politics, storytelling, place-making and creativity (Berry and Schleser 2014; Hjorth 2013, 2016). As Marsha Berry and Max Schleser (2014) observe in their collection on smartphone art and creative practice, mobile technologies are providing new ways for various disciplines such as filmmaking, screen writing and photography to reinvent themselves, their audiences and modes of engagement. In the marriage between the mobile and art, we see artists creating new types of cartographies and ways to imagine, visualise and practice place, quotidian narratives and embodiment. In turn, this phenomenon requires us to rethink how art is defined, curated, framed and contextualised. Mobile media affords new playful and reflexive practices that are shaping collaborations both inside and outside the artworld, as entangled within the often messy space of the everyday.

In sum, mobile art enables us to consider the role of the social and intimate as a medium through which to explore creative practice as a method and mode of knowledge transmission. As a tool for and of the intimate and social, mobile media as a vehicle for creative practice can take us into quotidian spaces and places. With this in mind, we sought to situate our findings from a three-year study into mobile games in Australian homes in a series of participatory workshops with young people. We asked young people to reflect upon the mobile games they played and adapt them to a physical space. This translation exercise from the digital to the offline required the young participant(s) to impart an embodied experience of digital game play into a physical version of corporeal play. Participants noted that the exercise changed how they related to mobile games and the intersection of game-based narratives with playful place-making practices.

GAMES OF BEING MOBILE: PLAY WORKSHOPS

In the first series of workshops at the Centre for Contemporary Photography (CCP) gallery in Melbourne we conducted ten workshops with school children aged from 7 to 16. We then conducted further workshops at the temporary public site MPavilion.[1] In these workshops we familiarised participant(s) with urban and physical games such as

PacManhattan (an urban street game where people dressed as PacMan and the game's ghosts, becoming "avatars" for players geo-located elsewhere who chase them around New York), flash-mobbing, the Massively Multiplayer Thumbwrestling game (a thumbwrestling exercise for groups) and the "New Arcade" or "indie" game scene.

We discussed the New Games movement of the 1970s, which encouraged all types of collective play in everyday life, and how this linked to other urban political movements like Situationist International that used techniques like "drifting" and non-conventional ways of moving through the city (such as *dérive*). These techniques have been appropriated by the New Arcade movement, which seeks to highlight the importance of the corporeal, social, physical and local in shaping how games are played. As a community of practice, the New Arcade is often referred to as "indie" gaming (Juul 2014; Simon 2012). The workshop sought to make participant(s) cognisant about the relationality between the digital and the material in making site-specific games and how innovative game movements have challenged and explored new ways of retelling our collective stories of the urban environment.

Then participant(s) worked in small collaborative groups to redesign, test and play a digital game they had adapted into a physical corporeal game. This process involved a lot of translation work. In each context—the gallery and the urban public space—the young people deployed different forms of play, storytelling and performance to rethink their mobile and digital media practices. Many of the children reflected that the play workshops had made them think differently about their videogame practices as well providing them a space to consider the significance of play in defining and narrating a sense of place.

In the series of MPavilion workshops with primary school children aged between 8 and 10 years old (around 120 participant(s) in February 2016, we sought to explore critically how participatory art can inform ethnographic methods and alternative modes of knowledge transmission in public urban spaces. These workshops were part of a performance and play intervention in which primary school children were asked to make site-specific games that responded to their digital play. As with the CCP workshops, we showed the young people examples of urban games—such as PacManhattan—that have effectively adapted digital games into urban spaces. We asked them to consider the differences between what constitutes "good play" in a digital space as opposed to physical space. The exercise not only asked participant(s) to design, test and perform their own games, but to consider the relationship between mobile media, play and storytelling (Fig. 8.1).

The MPavilion play workshops ran for two hours. After we began with warm-up flash mob game, the participant(s) then split into their groups. Participant(s) decided on a digital game to adapt into a physical game. They then tested, tweaked and adapted the game (which took up to forty-five minutes). The groups then reconvened and showed their games to the rest of the group (Fig. 8.2).

Over the course of the two hours, students adapted their digital mobile games to the non-digital context of MPavilion. Many students decided to make hybrid games like PacMan fused with Crossy Roads (which they called CrossyMan). Through the adaptation, designing and testing, students spoke about how digital components can and cannot be adapted to the material world. This exercise made them reflect upon what constitutes good mobile play and how ephemeral places such as MPavilion can be used as transformative play spaces. The activity

Fig. 8.1 Participants design their digital adaption for the urban park context

Fig. 8.2   The performance of play at MPavilion

effectively coalesced the participant(s)' experience of mobile games with urban play, such that they dynamically engaged in creating new stories of place infused with traces of their digital play.

CONCLUSION: THE POLITICS OF MOBILE PLAY AND URBAN FUTURES

The powerful role of play and its role in creating alternative stories of place has its tradition in urban play studies. Scholars such as de Souza e Silva (with Hjorth 2009) and de Lange (2015) have explored the role of hybrid or mixed reality games in renarrating and reframing our experience of place (Frissen et al. 2015). While all media interfaces could be said to be part of the "collective playful media landscape" (Frissen et al. 2015, p. 29), it is the mobile media device that exhibits and affords a capacity for play that can be carried around with us, thereby embedding playful place-making in the interstices of everyday life wherever we happen to be.

For de Lange (2015), play is enacted on, with and through the mobile as an increasingly illimitable platform that elicits playful communication and creativity. In Sicart's terms, mobile play happens in a "tangled world of people, things, spaces and cultures" (2014, p. 6). Within urban play scholarship (Frissen et al. 2015), play needs to be understood as part of the performance of place. Here place is taken in Massey's sense as "stories so far". It is through the performance of place that play gets enacted. We are also reminded of the important work by Sutton-Smith in which he highlights that play is intrinsically embedded with local cultural practices (1997).

In this chapter, we have focused on the relationship between mobile media, play and storytelling-as-place-making through a series of workshops that explored the entanglements of digital and corporeal play. The workshops deployed an innovative research approach to think critically through the possibilities of mobile play and urban futures. As tools for researching contemporary dynamics in action, mobile media can provide great insight into our storytelling and place-making practices. In particular, just as mobile media has always reinforced the role of place and locality, it can help to bring these concepts to the forefront.

NOTE

1. Melbourne, Australia. http://www.mpavilion.org/.

BIBLIOGRAPHY

Beaulieu, A. (2010). Research note: From co-location to co-presence: Shifts in the use of ethnography for the study of knowledge. *Social Studies of Science, 40*(3), 453–470. https://doi.org/10.1177/0306312709359219.

Berry, M., & Schleser, M. (Eds.). (2014). *Mobile Media Making in an Age of Smartphones.* New York: Palgrave Macmillan.

De Lange, M. (2015). *The playable city.* http://www.bijt.org/wordpress/wp-content/uploads/2015/06/150519_Michiel_de_Lange-STSM_report_Bristol.pdf.

de Souza e Silva, A. (2004). Art by telephone: From static to mobile interfaces. *Leonardo Electronic Almanac, 12*(10). http://mitpress2.mit.edu/e-journals/LEA/TEXT/Vol_12/lea_v12_n10.txt [accessed 4 January 2006].

de Souza e Silva, A., & Hjorth, L. (2009). Urban spaces as playful spaces: A historical approach to mobile urban games. *Simulation and Gaming, 40*(5), 602–625.

Frissen, V., et al. (2015). *Playful identities.* Amsterdam: Amsterdam University Press.

Hjorth, L. (2013). Stories of the mobile: Cartographies of the personal through a case study of mobile novels in Japan. In J. Freeman (Ed.), *Mobile media narratives* (pp. 238–248). Minnesota: University of Minnesota Press.

Hjorth, L. (2016). Narratives of ambient play: Camera phone practices in urban cartographies. In M. Foth, M. Brynskov, & T. Ojala (Eds.), *Citizen's right to the digital city: Urban interfaces, activism, and placemaking*. Singapore: Springer. ISBN 978-981-287-919.

Hjorth, L., & Byrne, L. (2016). *Design & play catalogue*. RMIT Design Hub.

Hjorth, L., & Richardson, I. (2014). *Gaming in locative, social and mobile media*. London: Palgrave.

Hjorth, L., King, N., & Kataoka, M. (Eds.). (2014). *Art in Asia-Pacific: Intimate publics*. New York: Routledge.

Hjorth, L., Pink, S., Sharp, K., & Williams, L. (2016). *Screen ecologies*. Cambridge, Mass: MIT Press.

Ito, M. (2003). Mobiles and the appropriation of place. *Receiver*, *8*. http://s3.amazonaws.com/academia.edu.documents/30697344/itoShort.pdf?AWSAccessKeyId=AKIAIWOWYYGZ2Y53UL3A&Expires=1491550558&Signature=2qnGUApxzSSMB0QphtRhhMSMNOs%3D&response-content-disposition=inline%3B%20filename%3DMobiles_and_the_appropriation_of_place.pdf [accessed 1 April 2017].

Juul, J. (2014). High-tech low-tech authenticity: The creation of independent style at the independent games festival. In *The 9th International Conference on the Foundations of Digital Games, FDG '14*.

Kato, F. (2014). Learning with mobile phones as research tools. In G. Goggin & L. Hjorth (Eds.), *The Routledge companion to mobile media*. London: Routledge.

Massey, D. (2005). *For space*. London: Sage.

Mizukoshi, S. (2003). Challenges and possibilities of Japan's media literacy: Perspectives of the MELL project. In *Media Education International Symposium: Korean Society for Journalism and Communication*, October 2, 2003.

Ozkul, D. (2014). Transforming cities, transforming locations: Locative media and sense of place. In A. de Souza e Silva & M. Sheller (Eds.), *Local and mobile: Edited collection*. New York: Routledge.

Perkins, C. (2009). Playing with maps. In M. Dodge, R. Kitchin, & C. Perkins (Eds.), *Rethinking maps* (pp. 167–188). Routledge: London.

Perkins, C. (2012). Playful mapping: The potential of a ludic approach. *International Cartographic Association Conference*. http://icaci.org/files/documents/ICC_proceedings/ICC2013/_extendedAbstract/121_proceeding.pdf.

Pink, S., & Hjorth, L. (2012). Emplaced cartographies: Reconceptualising camera phone practices in an age of locative media. *Media International Australia*, *145*, 145–156.

Raessens, J. (2006). Playful identities, or the ludification of culture. *Games & Culture*, 1(1), 52–57.

Rieser, M. (2011). *The mobile audiences: Media art and mobile technologies*. New York: ICI Global.

Sheller, M. (2014). Mobile art: Out of your pocket. In G. Goggin & L. Hjorth (Eds.), *The routledge companion to mobile media*.

Sicart, M. (2014). *Play matters*. Cambridge, MA: MIT Press.

Simon, B. (2012). Indie Eh? Some kind of game studies. *Loading…*, 7(11). http://journals.sfu.ca/loading/index.php/loading/article/view/129 [accessed 1 April 2017].

Sutton-Smith, B. (1997). *The ambiguity of play*. London: Routledge.

Verhoeff, N. (2012). Navigating screenspace: Towards performative cartography. In P. Snickars & P. Vonderau (Eds.), *Moving data: The iPhone and my media*. New York: Columbia University Press.

Verhoeff, N. (2013). *Mobile screens: The visual regime of navigation*. Amsterdam: Amsterdam University Press.

Wilmott, C. (2013). Cartographic city: Mobile mapping as a contemporary urban practice. *Refractory*. http://refractory.unimelb.edu.au/2012/12/28/wilmott/.

CHAPTER 9

Creating an Experiential Narrative: The Making of *Mobilarte*

Gerda Cammaer

Abstract This chapter uses the principles of the Slow Media Manifesto and Roland Barthes' punctum to contextualise and explain the making of *Mobilarte*. Shot in the city of Maputo (Mozambique) on an iPad, *Mobilarte* is an experiential video in three chapters. The video's narrative is non-verbal: all meaning is created in image and sound with the aim to recreate the actual experience of traveling the city by tuk-tuk and filming the trip on an iPad for the audience. The techniques used to achieve this were applying ideas about change blindness to the visual narrative and linking colour and sound for the audio. The production of the video is explained in detail as an example of mobile video art-making and of Slow Media creation.

Keywords Slow media · iPad filmmaking · Visual narrative

Maputo is the capital and largest city of Mozambique. Named after the river Maputo, the city is a large port on the Indian Ocean. It is also known as the City of Acacias because most of its large avenues and streets

---

G. Cammaer (✉)
School of Image Arts, Ryerson University, Toronto, Canada

© The Author(s) 2018
M. Schleser and M. Berry (eds.), *Mobile Story Making in an Age of Smartphones*, https://doi.org/10.1007/978-3-319-76795-6_9

are lined with acacia trees. Some of these streets mark the route I took through the city in a tuk-tuk (a three-wheeled motorised vehicle used as a taxi), which freely zigzagged through central and south Maputo, ending with a long drive along the Avenida da Marginal, a boulevard on the verge of the Indian Ocean. I filmed the three-hour ride on an iPad and made the three-part mobile video poem *Mobilarte* (12 minutes, 2014). The making of this video took me two years. As I wanted to edit the video so that it would be as close as possible to the original experience, I spent a long time experimenting with different editing techniques in image and sound. Most of my work is non-verbal: the story is told by the images and sounds without text or voice. My work is also experiential: I always try to recreate a lived experience (when filming) for the audience, which ironically usually implies doing a lot of post-production to approach as much as possible the sentiment of the raw image capture, its content and context. In the case of *Mobilarte*, the drive in a tuk-tuk, the impressions the city of Maputo left on me, and the experience of filming on an iPad while driving around are the three main elements that determined the final audio-visual narrative of the work.

MOBILARTE AND SLOW MEDIA CREATION

In *Mobile Media Making in an Age of Smartphones* (Berry and Schleser 2014) Patrick Kelly situates mobile filmmaking in the context of the Slow Media movement, more particularly the production of "media that generate a feeling that the particular medium belongs to just that moment of the user's life" (David et al. 2010 cited in Kelly 2014, p. 131). The Slow Media movement urges producers of media to create work that has auratic qualities, and for consumers to ingest such work accordingly (David et al. 2010; Kelly 2014): Slow Media cannot be consumed casually, but provoke the full concentration of their users. In retrospect, these ideas strongly resonate with my intensions when making *Mobilarte*.

Writing in *Camera Lucida*, Roland Barthes discusses the "punctum": whatever a photograph may contain that engages and "pricks" the viewer's subjectivity in a way that makes the image in question particularly of interest to him or her (Barthes 1981). As Barthes explains, often the punctum is a detail, or a partial object; in order to perceive a punctum, no analysis, except maybe memory, is of any use. "However lightning-like it may be, the punctum has, more or less potentiality, a power of expansion. This power is often metonymic" (Barthes 1981, p. 45). Finally, Barthes describes how the punctum is an addition: it is what we add to the image, yet it is always already there.

The punctum of an image can be hiding in the time and place when and where we captured the images. It was the detailed search for this in the footage of my tuk-tuk ride in Maputo and for ways to enhance the specific qualities of the iPad footage—a different kind of punctum—that made the post-production process of *Mobilarte* long and slow. I wanted to make sure that the video has (paraphrasing the Slow Media Manifesto) an aesthetically inspiring design and that it is suggestive of being unique yet also points beyond itself. Although I was not aware of this at the time, *Mobilarte* qualifies in multiple ways as a Slow Media creation, as it was "not about fast consumption but about choosing the ingredients mindfully and preparing them in a concentrated manner" (David et al. 2010). In what follows, I will describe in detail how these ideas and principles resonate with the creative process behind the experiential narrative of *Mobilarte*.

Capturing Images: Tuk-Tuking and iPadding the City

The advantage of travelling by tuk-tuk over travelling by foot is that you can cover a much larger area in a shorter amount of time. Compared to travelling by car, the benefit is that you are actually much closer to pedestrians and you can experience all the sounds and smells of the city, as well as the potholes. This all became part of the rather shaky hand-held aesthetic of *Mobilarte*. Filming the entire ride with an iPad as hand-held camera was awkward but fascinating, as the iPad is both camera and screen. iPad images also have interesting "motion blurs" when captured from a fast-moving vehicle: its camera cannot capture the motion at the speed that the vehicle is going, especially when filming lateral travelling shots of objects in close range. A good example is the rather messy look of the vegetation along the road in the third part of *Mobilarte* (*Maputo Praia*, or Maputo Beach), which makes for rather impressionistic painterly images contrary to a more *vérité* shooting style. Moreover, by changing the frame rate of the iPad footage in post-production from 30 to 24fps (film speed) I obtained ghost frames that give the video something of a haunted feel. This feature is an important aesthetic device in the second part of *Mobilarte* (*Maputo Baixa*, or Downtown Maputo), in which I tried to recreate my experience of feeling ill at ease in the more crowded and older part of the city, visualising a lingering sense of danger. Lastly, the iPad images were all affected by the way the winter light in Maputo was filtered by the dust in the air and by the lace-like patterned shadows created by the city's many acacia trees, something that features most prominently in the first part (titled *Maputo Alto*, or Uptown Maputo).

IMAGE EDITING AND THE CREATION OF A VISUAL NARRATIVE

The three different parts of *Mobilarte* each portray a different part of the city and tell a different story. The first part of the video, *Maputo Alto*, is more informative and in style closest to a typical travelogue. It is filmed in the neighbourhood around the central hospital of Maputo and its visual narrative tries to express two main features of the "Maputo experience": the fact that people constantly seem to appear out of nowhere and that in 2012 Maputo had become a city of mobile phone users. I achieved this by intercutting bystanders and pedestrians of similar street scenes in the extended neighbourhood into the three-street part of the tuk-tuk ride that serves as the visual guide-track for this part. Although this creates various jump-cuts, by cutting according to the similarities in the movement of the tuk-tuk, matching the inserted shots according to light (sun or shadow) and view (close-ups or wide shots), the flow of the video is not affected. I chose this particular style of figurative jump-cutting because it is the perfect illustration of how a combination of lived experience (what we see) and memory (what we expect to see) enhances change blindness or the inability to detect changes to an object or a scene in moving images across cuts. The overall effect is that even if some visual details and object or subject properties are not retained from one view to the next, when the images are edited and intercut this way we still perceive the ride as happening in a stable continuous world.

Change blindness is an interesting feature in moving images. Filmmakers are the natural experts in change blindness as they work with a rich body of knowledge about perception and vision and use this knowledge to do explicitly in a film what our visual system automatically does in reality: to combine a series of partial views (individual shots) into a coherent whole (a continuous scene) without audiences noticing the transitions (Simons and Levin 1997). The impression that I tried to convey by applying the principles of change blindness in editing was my experience of the busy city streets of Maputo, where people constantly seem to appear out of nowhere. To achieve this, I had to eliminate the many cars in the city. It is actually a disadvantage of travelling by tuk-tuk that parked cars dominate your tracking shots, which is not the case if one explores the city by foot. Yet, at times, I also used the cars to my advantage, and applied the same technique as above to speed up the action by intercutting cars of similar colours parked along the road. To compensate for the many cars that give the city a very western appearance I also created a scene showing only the more typical pushcarts and cut them based on the same principles of change blindness, combining carts that were filmed on different streets. The editing of the ride in uptown Maputo was further punctuated by focusing on the omnipresence of mobile phones and of publicity for mobile phones and calling cards, for example by using slow motion and inserting an advertisement for a mobile phone company.

The second part of *Mobilarte* takes place in the market area of downtown Maputo, a more crowded area with colourful displays of merchandise everywhere. Where in uptown Maputo most people seem to have a purpose (e.g. going home, going to work), in downtown Maputo people seem to hang around more, chatting, buying and selling. This experience—how all these bystanders leave an impression, and if or how that impression lingers—became the main focus of this part of *Mobilarte*. For the editing of this part, I mimicked how associative memory works, like constantly taking a second glance. This part thus became a continuous series of double takes, using both flash-backs and flash-forwards. Most of the shots in this part have been slowed down and because of the difference between the shooting rate (30fps) and the editing rate (24fps) at times a ghostly effect occurs: it looks like if people are followed by a Doppelgänger. This visual effect perfectly visualises the lingering of people, their images and my memories of that ride.

Another key moment in this part occurs when the iPad camera captured a sunbeam: a flare moves along the trajectory of the tuk-tuk, pointing out people on the pavement as if a higher power is at work, giving them an aura or a punctum of sorts. This beam of light allowed me to maintain continuity while cutting together shots that are not continuous: the movement of the flare makes it so that change blindness can do its wonders, enhancing the feeling of fleetingness that is already the main characteristic of this chapter. After a last turn around a corner, the tuk-tuk ride for this chapter ends with a slowed-down tracking shot along a crowded pavement full of vendors that is no longer intercut with repetitions of its own images, letting the ride make its own impression, and ending with a shot of people crossing the street along a puddle of water. The shot ends with a freeze-frame of a young man's t-shirt logo, which reads "lives". This can be interpreted as a reference to all the lives we have just come across.

The third part of *Mobilarte* is the most poetic and functions as a sigh of relief after experiencing the hustle and bustle in the city of Maputo itself. It is a trip to the beach and the long travelling shot along the Avenida da Marginal is almost kept as one continuous shot. Towards the end, when the shot is slowed down, it becomes a staggering image similar to those seen earlier in the film. This is due to the difference between the shooting and editing frame-rates (respectively 30 and 24fps), be it more pronounced this time. That the tuk-tuk is driving faster in this part has as effect that the low-resolution iPad images become more pixelated, creating impressionistic views of the vegetation along the road and the wide-open views on the beach, and the fabrics, dresses and African wax prints that are hanging in trees or on clotheslines along the road, on display for interested buyers. *Mobilarte* ends with an extremely slow-downed shot of tablecloths floating in the ocean breeze, as if they are waving us goodbye and are already pointing us in the direction of that moment when our visit to Maputo will be only a memory, a reminder that all moments (past or present) are fleeting memories in the making: "life is all memory, except for the one present moment that goes by you so quickly you hardly catch it going" (Tennessee Williams, cited in *Mobilarte*). While riding a tuk-tuk tends to make all present moments pass even faster, the iPad has proven to be a helpful tool to both catch them and to memorise them.

SOUND EDITING AND THE CREATION OF MOODS

The editing strategies for the images explained above were all carefully chosen with the purpose of recreating the experience of my tuk-tuk ride in Maputo, based on ideas about how (associative) memory and visual perception work. For the composition of the soundtrack I did something similar, but took this idea even further. In collaboration with sound artist Dafydd Hughes, soundtrack that is based on the four national colours of Mozambique—red, green, yellow and black—was composed. Hughes created four different notes by selecting very small portions of the original sound of the images, mostly the tuk-tuk sounds, that each were attributed to one of the four mentioned colours: higher notes for yellow and green; lower notes for red and black. He then wrote a special program that allowed the computer to scan the edited images of *Mobilarte* (similarly to how a squeegee would vertically pass over a window), creating a signal if one of the four national colours were hit or "switched on". This was another way actively to evoke Barthes' punctum. These signals were connected to the four notes created for the four colours and as such a Slow Mediaal composition was created for the first and last parts of *Mobilarte—Maputo Alto* and *Maputo Praia*.

In the first part, the soundtrack also includes some of the real sounds of the tuk-tuk, mostly when it slows down, speeds up or performs a manoeuvre. I considered it important to keep some of the original tuk-tuk sounds as they help the viewer to feel the movement of the vehicle and contribute to the more *cinema vérité* style of this first chapter. Part three, *Maputo Praia*, only has the sound of the tuk-tuk at the beginning of the ride: soon it is edited out to let the musical soundtrack be the sole sound. Here, the musical track was actually doubled up in editing, with a brief delay operating as an echo to itself, which contributes to the dreamy feel of this chapter and the expression of fleetingness. The second part of the video, *Maputo Baixa*, has a soundtrack that is a combination of two musical tracks. One is a collage of various parts of the sound created for part one, all played at only 30% of the speed. The other is a loop created by taking a small part of the sound of the first part also played at only 30% of the speed. Using the sound at only one third of its speed gives it a much lower pitch, making this part in the film stand out as the darkest. The effect of looping also contributes to this feeling, forcing us to consider the more mysterious and melancholic sides of this city, reminding us of its violent past as well as its current dangers.

CONCLUSION: IS *MOBILARTE* MOBILE ART?

In the introduction to the video the title *Mobilarte* is revealed as the name of an art framing shop in uptown Maputo, accidently filmed on my ride through the city. I found this an apt title for this video, and by extension for most of my work, which I consider to be a form of "mobile art": art videos filmed on a mobile device. I work with the specific technical aspects of the iPad camera, exploring and exploiting its own mobile-specific aesthetic, using this format as an alternative cultural form of expression. I could also have discussed *Mobilarte* as a city

Fig. 9.1   *Mobilarte* (2014), Gerda Cammaer

film by explaining how the piece portrays life in Maputo, but it seemed more useful to explain the piece's aesthetic qualities and all the artistic decisions made in the long process of producing it. In retrospect, this video also aligns itself very well with the Slow Media movement, which has gained importance in the past two decades, and thus I situated it within that framework. This was a useful exercise and even "slow" in it itself, as slow also means to be mindful and to be able to regard and to question one's own position from a different angle. *Mobilarte* was made a while ago now, and with this text I hope to bring it back to the attention of an interested audience. I hope that the video also has the tenth maxim of the Slow Media Manifesto as a characteristic: to be long lived and appear fresh even after years or decades. "Slow media do not lose their quality over time but at best get some patina that can even enhance their value" (David et al. 2010). In any case, besides being a slow media creation and slow in the making, *Mobilarte* is meant to be both mobile (made on the move) and moving (made to move), and mobile art (Fig. 9.1).

BIBLIOGRAPHY

Barthes, R. (1981). *Camera lucida: Reflections on photography* (R. Howard, Trans.). New York: Hill and Wang.

Berry, M., & Schleser, M. (Eds.). (2014). *Mobile media making in an age of smart phones.* New York: Palgrave Macmillan.

Cammaer, G. (2013/2014). *Mobilarte.* https://vimeo.com/90022219.

David, S., Jörg B., & Benedict, K. (2010, January 2). *The slow media manifesto.* Slow-Media.net. http://en.slow-media.net/manifesto.

Patrick, K. (2014). Slow media creation and the rise of instagram. In M. Berry & M. Schleser (Eds.), *Media making in an age of smartphones.* New York: Palgrave Macmillan.

Schutt, S., & Berry, M. (2011). The haunted photograph: Context, framing and the family story. *Current Narratives, 1*(3), 35–53.

Simons, D. J., & Levin, D. T. (1997). Change blindness. *Trends in Cognitive Sciences, 1*(7), 261–267.

CHAPTER 10

Mobile Virtual Realities and Portable Magic Circles

Michael Saker

Abstract Hybrid reality games such as Pokémon GO enable new approaches to embodied space that problematise traditional understandings of play. More recently, smartphones have again become involved in the provision of a new kind of relationship with space: the space of virtual reality. It is the intention of this exploratory chapter to examine mobile virtual reality as part of the continuum of mobile media in the context of two related themes: (1) physical distraction and (2) embodied space. The chapter will consider how this reassessment might provide new understandings of play's connection to the ordinary space of daily life before expanding upon these issues within the broader context of the "smartphone movement" and concluding with suggested directions for future research within the field.

Keywords AR · Augmented reality application · Mobile virtual reality

M. Saker (✉)
City University of London, London, UK

© The Author(s) 2018   97
M. Schleser and M. Berry (eds.), *Mobile Story Making in an Age of Smartphones*, https://doi.org/10.1007/978-3-319-76795-6_10

Following its release in July 2016, Pokémon GO became a global phenomenon. The game involves players using their smartphones to physically search for Pokémon that can be found within their environment. Once a Pokémon has been discovered, players must perform several tasks on their handset to capture it. In contrast to earlier Hybrid Reality Games (HRGs) such as Mogi (2004) and Foursquare (2009), Pokémon GO is an augmented reality (AR) application. Through a combination of smartphone camera and display, Pokémon appear on players' screens as if they are a part of the "real" world, "even if it is still a bit crude in phenomenological terms" (Licoppe 2016, p. 2). While the positive effects of this HRG—namely that players might spend more time outside—have been reported, the flipside of this discourse is more commonly publicised. Numerous accounts of accidents have emerged involving individuals who were so engrossed in the pursuit of Pokémon that they failed to take stock of their surroundings, in some cases proving fatal (Soble 2016).

As a corollary to this, locative games are still very much entangled in earlier apprehensions about mobile phones reducing the importance of space (de Souza e Silva and Frith 2010; Frith 2014, 2015) and the fear this physical dislocation may lead to injury. Yet, HRGs like Pokémon GO also have the potential to deepen, or enhance, connections to place and space. Studies in this field have demonstrated that locative media can elicit new approaches to sociality (Humphreys 2010), as well as new conceptions of embodiment (Evans and Saker 2017) precisely through the connectivity they enable. An important element of Pokémon GO and the provision of a new kind of space is therefore the transition to a mobile web. For de Souza e Silva (2006), a mixture of smartphones and the mobile web has led to what she refers to as "hybrid space". "This 'hybrid space' emerges when digital and physical spaces are joined, giving rise to new embodied experiences and social connections in place" (Saker and Evans 2016, p. 2). Significantly, these experiences are co-constructed through a confluence of digital locative information and the ambience of the city, which is neither temporally or spatially restricted.

For Hjorth and Richardson (2017), HRGs such as Pokémon GO "are manifestly ambient, as they become embedded in our daily routines, pedestrian movement, and interaction with the familiar strangers populating our neighbourhoods and urban spaces" (p. 5). However, in much the same way that smartphone camera applications can alter how place is communicated by allowing users to overlay images with faux-vintage filters (see Berry 2014), HRGs do not simply insert themselves into the daily customs of players, but more significantly modify how these individuals approach their circadian lives (Saker and Evans 2016). This observation is borne out of a growing body of research that has coalesced around mobile phones, locative media and the mediation of physical spaces since 2006 (Berry and Schleser 2014; de Souza e Silva and Frith 2010). Locative applications and pervasive forms of play can adjust the mobility choices of users, transforming their experiences of place (Gordon et al. 2013) and in some instances turning "ordinary life into a game" (Frith 2013). As Hjorth (2014) rightly notes, "what constitutes mobile gaming has changed dramatically" (p. 48). So too has our understanding of play (Saker and Evans 2016).

Conventionally speaking, the space of play has typically been theorised as cordoned off from ordinary life (Caillois 2001; Huizinga 1992). This marked sense of separation is most famously aligned to the work of Huizinga (1992) and his proposition that play interminably takes place within the "magic circle". When considering HRGs from this vantage point, the likes of Pokémon GO immediately present a different *kind* of play, one that involves a convergence of the two themes exegetically developed above through the history of mobile media, namely (1) physical distraction and (2) new embodied approaches to space. While issues surrounding HRGs and traditional understandings of play are indeed illuminating, and have been discussed at length elsewhere (Evans and Saker 2017; Saker and Evans 2016), this is not the focus of the chapter. Instead, what I am interested in exploring is how these two themes might be framed with the recent incorporation of virtual reality (VR) into smartphones, or mobile virtual reality (MVR) as I shall refer to it, and how this reassessment might provide an updated understanding of play and its connection to the ordinary space of daily life. In this vein, then, just as "selfies" can be understood as "a starting point to discuss self-reflexive and self-representation as a narrative within mobile filmmaking" (Schleser 2014, p. 149), MVR is very much positioned here as being part of the same continuum of mobile media that comprises locative applications, HRGs and AR.

MOBILE VIRTUAL REALITY (MVR), PHYSICAL DISTRACTION AND EMBODIED SPACE

In June 2014, Google released its first low-cost VR headset: Google Cardboard. With the aid of a fold-out cardboard viewer, users are effectively able to transform their smartphones into viable VR devices. This initial idea subsequently became the impetus for Google's more refined MVR platform, Daydream, which fundamentally does the same thing for

Daydream-ready phones. Suitable handsets can be placed inside Google's accompanying headset, the Daydream View, and then paired with a wireless controller that is replete with smart sensors that read physical movements and gestures. Further, Google plans on "launching standalone Daydream headsets with select hardware partners" (Faulker and Osbourne 2017) at some point soon. In terms of its commercial positioning, Daydream is very much presented as a tool of escape, as a way of leaving one's environment behind and being transported to somewhere more exciting. Daydream ostensibly functions in the following ways: first, as a way of exploring new worlds, such as "famous museums, far-away cities, other planets and beyond"; second, as a personal cinema, where users can watch "films on a virtual big screen", as well as experience sports and concerts as if they were "actually there"; third, as a new and more immersive form of gameplay, where the controller puts players right into the action (Google VR 2017).

The multiple applications of MVR are at present being explored by a growing number of industries. Indeed, MVR has been used to offer terminally ill patients the experience of being outside (Murphy 2017), to broaden the atmosphere of music festivals like Coachella (Locke 2017) and to allow home buyers to take virtual tours of properties without the need to leave their own homes. At the same time, stories have also emerged examining MRV's impact on public spaces (see Walker 2015) and its penchant for leaving users potentially vulnerable to injury. A good case in point involves a well-publicised account of a man playing a MVR game on his morning commute to work (see Patel 2016) and the commotion this caused with other passengers. Not only was this incident widely reported, but it was done so from the perspective of embodied space and the fact the man in question was very much separated from his physical environment. So, what does this suggest about MVR usage and its relationship to space?

MVR evidently involves a different kind of engagement with space than earlier mobile devices, HRGs and AR applications. Studies in this context have examined the propensity of mobile devices physically to distract individuals from their immediate surroundings (Gergen 2002; Katz and Aahus 2002). Research has demonstrated that mobile phone usage can be linked to all manner of accidents in public spaces (Lamberg and Muratori 2012; Stavrinos et al. 2011). Because of this, a common tactic for walkers navigating any urban environment is to be vigilant of individuals who are too busy looking at their mobile phones than to notice that they are about to collide with an oncoming passer-by. While MVR does involve some physical effort, with head movement translated into digital movement, alongside wireless controllers serving as an intermediary for hand gestures and so on, mobility is nonetheless limited. This is precisely because MVR necessarily prohibits users from seeing the physical space that surrounds them. Instead what they perceive is the digital vista simulated within their headsets. Correlatively, individuals are more likely to use MVR in those public spaces that are "fuzzy spaces", such as commuting on a train, as demonstrated above. In this vein, then, much like mobile media, MVR provides users with some degree of control over the interactions they might have. Not that this is a new thing. As de Souza e Silva and Frith (2010) point out, people have always attempted to control their immediate surroundings. Reading, for instance, allows a level of physical dislocation (Schilvelbusch 1986), just as personal music players can create personalised "soundscapes". In a similar vein, and as touched on above, HGRs like Pokémon GO are equally predicated on users' attention shifting between two different but interrelated activities. Yet, the affordances of MVR notably differ from these examples.

MVR usage does not implicate the senses moving between two different perceptions of space, both co-constructed through a confluence of physical and digital interactions. Instead, MVR usage facilitates the separation and synthesis of the senses. The sights and sounds experienced by users are simulated within their headsets, while their physicality is effectually incorporated into the overall experience. Put differently, while HRGs involve the physical incorporating the digital, in this instance it is the digital that incorporates the physical. In turn, MVR seemingly moves beyond de Souza e Silva's (2006) "hybrid space", as well as Hjorth and Richardson's (2017) notion of "ambient play", and towards something more anastomotic. The embodied space of MVR is not centred on "hybrid space" and the oscillation between differing modes of attention and distraction, but rather a physical experience that is better described as "hybrid presence". This hybrid presence occurs when MVR users occupy two different spaces that are ceaselessly experienced as being one. The virtual world does not end until the headset is removed, nor is it divided. As a result, it is not so much that MVR usage reduces the importance of physical space per se, but more significantly MVR attempts to remove the perception of physical space altogether, or rather physical space is absorbed by the digital. Symptomatic of this, surrounding discourses have begun to include apprehensions about the kind of physical vulnerability "hybrid presence" might produce, as seen in the reporting of the man playing MVR on his way to work, just as this form of embodied space equally suggests an updated approach to play that is noteworthy in the context of mobile media.

For Evans and Saker (2017), a way of understanding the subject experience of HRGs, such as the location-based social networking site Foursquare, can be comprehended through their conceptual figure, the "playeur", which builds on Humphreys' (2010) study of the mobile social networking site Dodgeball in conjunction with de Souza e Silva and Hjorth's (2009) understanding of the flâneur and Luke's (2006) dystopian "phoneur". "For the 'playeur' ordinary space is no longer simply 'ordinary', nor is it only a space of consumption, but is also playful and open to engagement" (Saker and Evans 2016, p. 12). Accordingly, traditional boundaries between ordinary life and play are effectively challenged. In contrast to this, MVR involves a different interpretation of play's delineation from normal space. Ordinary space, from this position, is not so much overlaid with play, but rather circumvented through a prioritising of the digital. In this vein, MVR does more than offer a window on the world; significantly, MVR provides a digital doorway to innumerable realms that can be playfully experienced at any time and in any place. In the context of the magic circles, then, MVR elicits an approach to play that is necessarily distinct from ordinary space. When the headset is on, the outside world disappears, and there is something magical about this experience. Users are effectively able to carry multiple worlds in their pockets, which can be called upon, for instance, to transcend the distinct lack of space felt while travelling to work on a crammed train (see Walker 2015). While Huizinga's (1992) "magic circle" might be challenged in the milieu of HRGs, and rightly so, it is notably affirmed when examined in the context of MVR.

DISCUSSION

Throughout this chapter, MVR has been positioned as a recent development within the field of mobile media that builds on surrounding themes of physical distraction and embodied space. As a way of beginning to understand the kind of embodied space MVR configures, I have suggested the notion of "hybrid presence". To be clear, "hybrid presence" is not built on differing modes of attention and distraction per se, but rather a process of anastomosis, and through this the separation and synthesis of the senses. Within the context of play, such siloing suggests another way of comprehending this phenomenon and its connection to ordinary life. Whereas the likes of Pokémon Go challenges Huizinga's "magic circle", MVR presents an understanding of play that is not so much experienced within the space of ordinary life, but rather through its denial. Because of this, questions should be asked about emerging divisions between public and private, as well as the phenomenology of this kind of physical experience, and its impact on sociality. While there is not the space to adequately tackle these questions here, it is my intention that this chapter will serve as a suitable primer for future research in the area of MVR, just as it should help underline its place in the wider context of the "mobile movement" (see Berry and Schleser 2014).

BIBLIOGRAPHY

Berry, M. (2014). Filtered smartphone moments: Haunting places. In *Mobile media making in an age of smartphones* (pp. 58–67). New York: Palgrave Macmillan.

Berry, M., & Schleser, M. (Eds.). (2014). *Mobile media making in an age of smartphones*. Berlin: Springer.

Caillois, R. (2001). *Man, play and games*. Champaign, IL: University of Illinois Press [Original work published 1958].

de Souza e Silva, A. (2006). From cyber to hybrid: Mobile technologies as interfaces of hybrid spaces. *Space & Culture, 9*(3), 261–278.

de Souza e Silva, A., & Frith, J. (2010). Locational privacy in public spaces: Media discourses on location-aware mobile technologies. *Communication, Culture and Critique, 3*(4), 503–525.

Evans, L., & Saker, M. (2017). *Location-based social media: Space, time and identity*. Berlin: Springer.

Faulkner, C., & Osbourne, J. (2017). Google Daydream news, features and everything you need to know. *Techradar.* http://www.techradar.com/news/phone-and-communications/mobile-phones/android-vr-release-date-news-features-1321245.

Frank, A. (2016). *Six Pokémon GO tips for the ultimate beginner*. Retrieved from http://www.polygon.com/2016/7/9/12136310/Pokémon-GO-tips-how-to-play-beginners.

Frith, J. (2012). Splintered space: Hybrid spaces and differential mobility. *Mobilities, 7*(1), 131–149.

Frith, J. (2013). Turning life into a game: Foursquare, gamification, and personal mobility. *Mobile Media & Communication, 1*(2), 248–262.

Frith, J. (2014). Communicating through location: The understood meaning of the Foursquare check-in. *Journal of Computer-Mediated Communication, 19*(4), 890–905.

Frith, J. (2015). *Smartphones as locative media*. London: Polity Press.

Gergen, K. (2002). The challenge of absent presence. In J. Katz & M. Aakhus (Eds.), *Perpetual contact: Mobile communication, private talk, public performance* (pp. 227–241). New York: Cambridge University Press.

Google VR. (2017). *Introducing Daydream*. https://vr.google.com/daydream/ [accessed 17 August 2017].

Gordon, E., Baldwin-Philippi, J., & Balestra, M. (2013). Why we engage: How theories of human behavior contribute to our understanding of civic engagement in a digital era. *Berkman Center Research Publication, 21*, 1–29.

Hjorth, L. (2014). Co-present and ambient play: A case study of mobile gaming. In *Mobile media making in an age of smartphones* (pp. 48–57). New York: Palgrave Macmillan.

Hjorth, L., & Richardson, I. (2014). *Gaming in social, locative and mobile media*. Berlin: Springer.

Hjorth, L., & Richardson, I. (2017). Pokémon GO: Mobile media play, place-making, and the digital wayfarer. *Mobile Media & Communication, 5*(1), 3–14.

Huizinga, J. H. (1992). *Homo ludens: A study of the play-element in culture*. Boston: Beacon Press (original work published 1938).

Humphreys, L. (2010). Mobile social networks and urban public space. *New Media & Society, 12*, 763–778.

Katz, J., & Aahkus, M. (2002). *Perpetual contact: Mobile communication, private talk, public performance*. Cambridge: Cambridge University Press.

Lamberg, E. M., & Muratori, L. M. (2012). Cell phones change the way we walk. *Gait & Posture, 35*(4), 688–690.

Licoppe, C. (2016). From Mogi to Pokémon GO: Continuities and change in location-aware collection games. *Mobile Media & Communication, 5*(1), 1–6.

Locke, C. (2017, April 25). Take a trip inside Coachella's psychedelic 120-foot VR dome. *Wired*. https://www.wired.com/2017/04/coachella-psychedelic-vr-dome/.

Luke, R. (2006). The phoneur: Mobile commerce and the digital pedagogies of the wireless web. In P. Trifonas (Ed.), *Communities of difference: Culture, language, technology* (pp. 185–204). London: Palgrave Macmillan.

Murphy, M. (2017, May 3). Black Mirror: Virtual reality headsets given to terminally ill patients so they can enter computer simulations during their final days. *The Sun*. https://www.thesun.co.uk/tech/3464454/virtual-reality-headsets-given-to-terminally-ill-patients-so-they-can-enter-computer-simulations-during-their-final-days/.

Patel, J. (2016). VR headsets: Is this what commuting will look like in the future. *BBC Newsbeat*. http://www.bbc.co.uk/newsbeat/article/35972449/vr-headsets-is-this-what-commuting-will-look-like-in-the-future.

Rosenberg, E. (2016, August 22). In a safeguard for children, some civil liberties groups see concerns. *The New York Times*, p. 14.

Saker, M., & Evans, L. (2016). Everyday life and locative play: An exploration of Foursquare and playful engagements with space and place. *Media, Culture & Society, 38*(8), 1–15.

Schilvelbusch, W. (1986). *The railway journey: The industrialization of time and space in the 19th century*. Los Angeles: University of California Press.

Schleser, M. (2014). Connecting through mobile autobiographies: Self-reflexive mobile filmmaking, self-representation, and selfies. In *Mobile media making in an age of smartphones* (pp. 148–158). New York: Palgrave Macmillan.

Soble, J. (2016, August 25). Driver in Japan playing *Pokémon GO* kills pedestrian. *The New York Times*, p. 2.

Stavrinos, D., Byington, K. W., & Schwebel, D. C. (2011). Distracted walking: Cell phones increase injury risk for college pedestrians. *Journal of Safety Research, 42*(2), 101–107.

Walker, A. (2015, November 6). That VR guy riding the subway now with video update: We found him. *Gizmodo*. http://gizmodo.com/that-vr-guy-riding-the-subway-now-with-exclusive-video-1710731241.

CHAPTER 11

New Contextualised Perspectives: Using Bluetooth Beacons and Drones for Mixed-Reality Storytelling

Patrick Kelly

Abstract The ubiquity of smartphones has led to a shift in the way that content is created and consumed. This shift allows media makers to tell mixed-reality documentary stories that are highly contextualised to various places and that offer new perspectives on those places, thereby creating exciting, new contexts and auratic experiences. This chapter offers an insight into the creation of such projects by using a practice-based research approach to examine the development of a mobile walking tour app in partnership with Winda Mara Aboriginal Corporation in western Victoria, Australia. The app augments the Tyrendarra Indigenous Protected Area (IPA) to provide visitors with a glimpse of Gunditjmara culture and history, including its prominence in Australian Indigenous knowledge as "one of Australia's earliest and largest aquaculture ventures" (Victorian Department of the Environment, Tyrendarra indigenous protected area, 2003).

Keywords Mobile app · Mixed-reality experiences · Tyrendarra indigenous protected area (IPA)

P. Kelly (✉)
RMIT University, Melbourne, Australia

© The Author(s) 2018
M. Schleser and M. Berry (eds.), *Mobile Story Making in an Age of Smartphones*, https://doi.org/10.1007/978-3-319-76795-6_11

Kerrigan and McIntyre suggest that "a creative research approach that investigates acts and contexts of creation, as well as exposing tacit and explicit demonstrations of skills, knowledge and methods of documentary practice could help researchers to tease out the creative forces that are at work for documentary practitioners" (2010, p. 126). This project has been a sojourn from the Instagram work discussed in my chapter in the previous volume, *Mobile Media Making in an Age of Smartphones* (Berry and Schleser 2014), which explored much more individual "acts and contexts of creation", namely the use of existing mobile applications for Slow Media production of personal stories (Kelly 2014, pp. 129–138). Similarly, the Tyrendarra Indigenous Protected Area (IPA) app is a project that is significantly affected by the contexts around its creation. A collaborative project between Winda Mara Aboriginal Corporation, postgraduate Media students from RMIT University, the author as an executive producer and a teacher to the students, as well as app developers and a drone pilot, each aspect of the collaboration has its own significance and impact on the resulting product. While there are several significant areas to explore within this project, in terms of examining it as a tertiary Work Integrated Learning (WIL) project model, or as a creative collaboration with Aboriginal partners, this chapter will instead examine the project's significance as a creative practice process and outcome. Carole Gray offers some key principles that are central to this approach.

> Firstly, research which is initiated in practice, where questions, problems, challenges are identified and formed by the needs of practice and practitioners; and secondly, that the research strategy is carried out through practice, using predominantly methodologies and specific methods familiar to us as practitioners. (Gray 1996, p. 3)

In this way, the research conducted about the content, style and technology of this project—the three key creative components to any media work—was all undertaken with the end point of the release of this mobile app as our goal. This research was conducted within a collaborative professional context that utilised mixed reality storytelling for mobile media, drone videography and remote telecommunications as some of its key methods, affordances and constraints. In particular, the implications of the project's use of Bluetooth Beacons, mobile media, and drone video and still images in relation to auratic storytelling practices make it a significant case study.

Using Mobile Devices for Mixed-Reality Experiences

Mobile devices are increasingly diversifying the way in which stories can be told. Creative media projects that utilise "novel combinations of ubiquitous technology can flourish in the gaps helping to create 'new shadows and opacities" (Berry and Hamilton 2010, p. 53), augmenting various places. The use of locative functionality in mobile storytelling means that stories can be contextualised to specific locations, offering users what Milgram and Kishino (1994) refer to as a mixed-reality experience that offers additional information and perspectives across real and virtual environments that cannot be had otherwise. Bolter et al. write that "in mixed-reality (MR) applications, the computer provides digital information that is integrated into the user's view of the physical environment" (Bolter et al. 2006, p. 22). With the Tyrendarra IPA mixed-reality app, users can watch and listen to media content that integrates into their experience of this place.

The app uses Bluetooth Beacons at eight checkpoints along the Tyrendarra IPA circuit. With the app installed and Bluetooth enabled on their personal mobile device, users can watch, listen to and read content when it is automatically triggered by the Beacons at these checkpoints. The content in the app includes still video and still images that highlight significant features around each checkpoint and relate to the story being told aurally by various Gunditjmara elders and rangers about the place on which the visitor stands. These stories aim to provide some additional context to the Indigenous Protected Area for visitors whilst not taking away the possibility that visitors might join a "physical tour" (i.e. one led by a Budj Bim Tours guide, face to face).

The content was mostly created during a field trip by RMIT postgraduate media students with the direction of Ms. Eileen Alberts, a Gunditjmara Elder and mentor for the Winda Mara Aboriginal Corporation's Land Management Program, and Budj Bim Tours, and of the author.

In addition to the audio-visual material produced by the students, drone footage was later recorded of the Tyrendarra IPA for the project by a drone cinematographer. We sought this footage to increase the value of the content and of the app itself. With reference to range of practices, including the use of drone video, Dean Keep writes that "it's worth considering how portable digital media devices may be reconfiguring traditional approaches to both film and video production"

(Keep 2015, p. 6). He points to filmmaker Adam Bhala Lough, who declares "Helicopter shots, slow motion car mounts, under water scenes: you can shoot all of these by yourself and effectively raise your production value. It's an indie filmmaker's dream" (Bhala Lough 2014, n.p.; Keep 2015) (Fig. 11.1).

In addition to raising the production value of the project, the inclusion of drone footage also allows visitors to view the area from a new vantage point. Drone filmmaker Jay Worsley, while discussing his aptly titled film *Perspective* (2016), points to the new outlook on a familiar place that can be achieved when using accessible drone technology for video production. He says:

> being able to see the forest that they see all the time but seeing it from a different angle and a different perspective'cause it gives you a different feeling—different emotion—just by changing how you view it [...] Drones are able to get so many different angles that we wouldn't get before, so [...] seeing that forest that everybody's been in—there's a forest in Flagstaff that's in *Perspective* that I've been to a tonne of times but I had no idea just how it looked when I was 200 feet in the air; being able to see so much more of it; being able to see how the mountains are carved through the trees [...] and it makes it new and fresh to me. (Worsley in Airvuz 2017, n.p.)

While the drone footage offers visitors a new vantage point at Tyrendarra IPA, the use of Bluetooth Beacons allow for granular, localised and highly contextualised stories to be told at each checkpoint around the walking circuit. For example, when users reach the tumuli (stacks of volcanic rock) towards the back end of the Tyrendarra IPA circuit, they are told the story of the eruption of Budj Bim and the creation of the lava flow that gave life to Gunditjmara country, allowing for the creation of one of Australia's largest and earliest aquaculture systems (Victorian Department of the Environment 2003, n.p.). The tumuli, while spectacular on their own, become much more significant to visitors when the context surrounding the interwoven connection between the lava flow and the Gunditjmara becomes known. The app provides users with an explicit context for this location, telling the story of this specific place, and giving visitors a glimpse at how significant it is, or some sense of aura (Fig. 11.2).

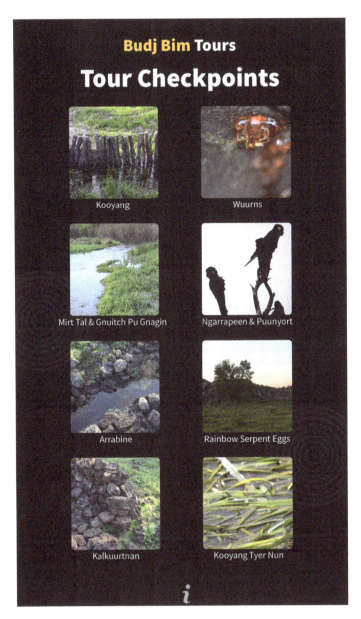

Fig. 11.1 Screengrab of Tyrendarra IPA mobile app checkpoints screen

Fig. 11.2   Still from Tyrendarra IPA mobile app. Drone image of Tumuli

CONCEPTUAL AND TECHNICAL LIMITATIONS OF THE PROJECT

I purport that the discovery of various contexts provided through mobile devices for mixed-reality documentary storytelling can provoke such auratic experiences at places like the Tyrendarra IPA. But while Schutt and Berry (2011) make the case that these different intensities may be hiding in the media object itself, in their case a photograph, in the case of the Tyrendarra IPA Trails project, I believe that the different intensity experienced by a visitor occurs in relation to the place and not in the app itself. The app acts as a vessel to make explicit the context of the place to the visitor, but it is in the place itself that the visitor feels that significance.

Bolter et al. point to the aura that a mixed-reality project can inspire in a user of such a project when they are experiencing the work at the intended location. They point to their own project, The Voices of Oakland, a mixed-reality, audio experience based at Oakland Cemetery that told dramatic stories of the history of Atlanta, Georgia, through the perspective of those who lived it, who are now buried at the cemetery (Dow et al. 2005). They write:

> In the Oakland Cemetery, for example, a physical tour of the cemetery should be high in aura, and a tour supported by augmented reality perhaps equally high. Because both the human-guided tour and the augmented

> tour maintain the user's physical connection to the site, the experience
> will be felt as unique. Physical presence should enhance the aura. In this
> respect, MR experiences should be more effective at conveying aura than
> other media forms. (Bolter et al. 2006, p. 29)

I suggest that listening to and seeing the media content in the Tyrendarra IPA app whilst being physically present at the Tyrendarra IPA location should enhance the aura; however, I would stop short of purporting that the auratic experience would be equal to a physical tour of the site, as led by one of the Gunditjmara Elders, rangers or tour staff. This is due to the personal context that is often conveyed on such a tour.

A technical challenge faced in the development of the app was a result of the remote location of the Tyrendarra IPA, which pertained to the limitation of file sizes and data limits, restricting the amount and bit-rate of the media that was included in the app. In most circumstances, the media files could be stored on a Content Management System and temporarily downloaded by the user on request; however, the remote location of the Tyrendarra IPA means that 4G/3G mobile data coverage is patchy, especially at the rear of the area, and therefore the media content is best embedded in the app in order for ease of access.

With the content now embedded, the total size of the app increased significantly. It was necessary to try to limit the total size to below 100 mb, which in 2017 was Apple's over-the-air download limit for an app of this type (Kumparak 2015). While the intention originally was to include a one- to two-minute video at each of the eight checkpoints, this would mean that the size of the app (even with each video at 4–5 mb when compressed), in terms of data, would balloon out to a size likely deemed unfeasible by Apple. Unfortunately, this meant that only one video was embedded in the app, at the first checkpoint, with still images and audio making up the bulk of the content for the subsequent checkpoints. Likewise, in order to limit the size of the audio files for the stories at each checkpoint, the bit rate of the audio was limited to 128 kbps (taking the size of each file from ~14 mb to ~130 kb), which is not ideal but also not unreasonable, especially considering that the average listener is accessing the audio at an exterior rural location. We hope to upgrade these features in subsequent versions of the app as technology develops.

These technical limitations, while frustrating, also act as reminder of how far we have come. I refer to Mollison's (2003) recommendation that the 80 gb storage space afforded by an external hard drive "is a good option for [...] longer projects" (p. 162). In 2017, the standard for external hard drives in video production was at least a couple of ter-abytes (TB). So, while we may be unfortunately still limited technically at times, it is encouraging that the conceptual framework for delivering these sorts of projects is developed enough to deliver a highly contextu-alised storytelling experience to visitors of such a site. Nonetheless, the creative team look forward to further investment in the technological infrastructure at such locations by government and business alike.

CONCLUSION

It is through working within a professional context that has its own unique affordances and constraints that new knowledge about creative media practices can emerge. By analysing the processes and outcomes of producing the Tyrendarra IPA mobile app project, it can be understood that the combination of various technologies, including mobile applica-tions, Bluetooth Beacons and drone videography, can be utilised to cre-ate mixed-reality documentary storytelling projects that augment places and enable auratic experiences by providing additional contexts to vis-itors. While this project required that the amount of content and con-text created was restrained for various reasons, such a scalable framework could be used for a much larger project that offers an expanded amount of content and context for a place, thereby invoking a feeling of a "dif-ferent intensity" about a place.

Acknowledgements The author wishes to acknowledge the contributions to this project work by Eileen Alberts, Jody Agnew, Aaron Morgan, Matthew Butt, the Winda Mara Aboriginal Corporation's Land Management Program, Budj Bim Tours, Bruce Partland, Solly De Silva, Opie Sayner-Hassall, Julian Grant, Shamir Muhammad, Emma Sharp and Kaifeng Wang.

REFERENCES

Airvuz. (2017). *The Drone Dish: Jay Worsley [Video]*. Retrieved from https://www.airvuz.com/video/The-Drone-Dish-Jay-Worsley?id=58dd5517cdad787c3ac6e1ad.

Berry, M., & Hamilton, M. (2010). Mobile computing applications: Bluetooth for local voices. *Journal of Urban Technology, 17*(2), 37–55. https://doi.org/10.1080/10630732.2010.515084.

Berry, M., & Schleser, M. (2014). *Mobile media making in an age of smart-phones.* New York: Palgrave Macmillan. https://doi.org/10.1057/9781137469816.0018.

Bhala Lough, A. (2014). Why independent filmmakers should embrace GoPro (and Vice Versa). *Filmmaker Magazine.* Retrieved from http://filmmakermagazine.com/87934-why-independent-filmmakers-shouldembrace-gopro-and-vice-versa/#.VVPuk2thiSM.

Bolter, J. D., MacIntyre, B., Gandy, M., & Schweitzer, P. (2006). New media and the permanent crisis of Aura. *The International Journal of Research into New Media Technologies, 12*(1), 21–39. https://doi.org/10.1177/1354856506061550.

Dow, S., Lee, J., Oezbek, C., MacIntyre, B., Bolter, J. D., & Gandy, M. (2005). *Exploring spatial narratives and mixed reality experiences in Oakland cemetery.* Paper presented at the Proceedings of the 2005 ACM SIGCHI International Conference on Advances in Computer Entertainment Technology, Valencia, Spain.

Gray, C. (1996). Inquiry through practice: Developing appropriate research strategies. In P. Korvenmaa (Ed.), *No guru, no method conference proceedings.* Research Institute, University of Art and Design. http://carolegray.net/Papers%20PDFs/ngnm.pdf.

Keep, D. (2015). From Barbie video girl to smartphones: How portable media devices are shaping new screen production practices. In *ASPERA annual conference 2015: Whats this space? Screen practice, audiences and education for the future decade.* Flinders University, Adelaide, Australia. Retrieved from https://www.academia.edu/19533845/From_Barbie_Video_Girl_to_Smartphones_How_portable_media_devices_are_shaping_new_screen_production_practices.

Kelly, P. (2014). Slow media creation and the rise of instagram. In *Mobile media making in an age of smartphones* (pp. 129–138). New York: Palgrave Macmillan.

Kerrigan, S., & McIntyre, P. (2010). The creative treatment of actuality: Rationalizing and reconceptualizing the notion of creativity for documentary practice. *Journal of Media Practice, 11*(2), 111–130. https://doi.org/10.1386/jmpr.11.2.111_1.

Kumparak, G. (2015). iOS apps can now be twice as big. *TechCrunch.* https://techcrunch.com/2015/02/12/ios-app-size-limit/ [accessed 12 February].

Milgram, P., & Kishino, F. (1994). Augmented reality: A class of displays on the reality-virtuality continuum. *SPIE,* 282–292.

Mollison, M. (2003). *Producing videos: A complete guide* (2nd ed.). Crows Nest, NSW: Allen & Unwin.

Schutt, S., & Berry, M. (2011). The haunted photograph: Context, framing and the family story. *Current Narratives, 3,* 35–53. Retrieved from http://ro.uow.edu.au/currentnarratives/vol1/iss3/6.

Victorian Department of Environment. (2003). *Tyrendarra indigenous protected area*. Retrieved from https://www.environment.gov.au/indigenous/ipa/declared/tyrendarra.html.

Worsley, J. (2016). *Perspective [Video]*. Retreived from https://vimeo.com/166441527.

CHAPTER 12

Interface Is the Place: Augmented Reality and the Phenomena of Smartphone–Spacetime

Rewa Wright

Abstract This chapter explores the emergent field of mobile augmented reality (AR) art as articulated on smartphones and tablets, and the impact of these new technologies on participatory art practices. Examples for analysis are drawn from recent geo-located mobile art by influential practitioners J. C. Freeman, J. Cardiff and G. B. Miller, W. Pappenheimer and T. Thiel. All have recently produced smartphone art apps and mobile AR apps that advance the concept of a parallel reality to the real world. These artworks are examined to articulate further the technical processes that produce art as a differentiated socio-cultural experience to the conventional gallery-based model of spectatorship. This chapter argues that this experience sits within the emergent field of posthuman digital humanities, as discussed by the eminent theorist Rosi Braidotti (2013).

Keywords Augmented reality · Smartphone-spacetime

R. Wright (✉)
UNSW Art and Design, University of New South Wales, Sydney, Australia

© The Author(s) 2018   117
M. Schleser and M. Berry (eds.), *Mobile Story Making in an Age of Smartphones*, https://doi.org/10.1007/978-3-319-76795-6_12

From an engineering perspective, touch capacitance activates the smart-phone screen as a control surface. Since the human body is needed to close the circuit, the smartphone screen differs from regular screens in that it does not operate alone. This articulates a special case of the interface, where the screen itself is always linked to a user through the physical gestures of plac-ing one's finger on the control surface. Rather than perceiving smartphones as tools that allow humans to operate as media-producing beings in a place, I draw on conceptual developments in mathematics and physics to propose that due to their unique technical interface, which uses capacitive touch to affectively conjoin the body of user to the device, smartphones have become an actual place. This cultural shift has occurred in part through the bodily connection between the user of a phone and the device itself.

When we view an interface as a place, the act of "placing" comes to the fore. Techniques of placing, developed by computer engineers, have a critical impact on the interface. The concept of *locus* (Latin for "place") is at the heart of geometry, a field that is responsible for developing the protocols around the placement of coordinates in virtual (and real) space. Understood in mathematics as a "set of points", in the context of smartphone software, locus shapes the capacity of computer vision applications to track and situate camera deployed image streams on to the physical world. The technical procedures that produce locus in aug-mented reality (AR) rely on coordinates of placement in conjunction with hybrid human–machine techniques of placing, using sensors such as the accelerometer and gyroscope, synchronously track the phone so as to elicit positional awareness for the subject.

Drawing on Albert Einstein's view of spacetime, where objects exist within an "inertial frame of reference"—all bodies move together and there is no temporal dislocation (Special Theory of Relativity 1905)—I propose the analogous theory of smartphone–spacetime as an articu-lation of an emergent spatio-temporal modality where the smartphone is considered as a locus connecting virtual and physical and conjoining this matter in a synchronous configuration, arranged through the agen-tial relations of software, algorithms and code.

From Spacetime to Smartphone–Spacetime

The theme of a parallel sense of reality, an ambient topology that stretches across the regular geography of the physical world, has been explored at a more serious and socially conscious level for some time by artists creating art on mobile phones. Artworks such *The City of Forking Paths* (Cardiff and Miller 2014) used a bespoke geo-fenced app to situate participants in a unique experience of a parallel reality (Wright 2014a, 2015). During the walk's sixty-six minutes, and available only after dusk, one followed the directions given by Cardiff's binaurally recorded voice and was asked to watch the smartphone screen at the same time. The concept was to apprehend two worlds happening in tandem: firstly, the real world in which the walk took place, at night, along Circular Quay and through the atmospherically spooky back alleys of the Rocks and Miller's Point; secondly, the parallel world conveyed in the film shot by Cardiff and Miller at those same locations. The participants, watching the film as they walk, follow a meandering yet deftly crafted narrative that begins by describing Sydney's historical past, then move on to present concerns such as the development of the Miller's Point area and the displacement of long-time residents to make way for luxury apartments.

Perceptually, participants were asked to follow both virtual and actual trajectories at the same time, and this act of trying to follow both performs a number of perceptual tricks. Since the film is shot so as to mirror the exact locations that the participant is walking around, the actual environment is enfolded as a virtual double. When you witness, on screen, a gagged man in a straightjacket walking toward you, involuntarily, your proprioceptive sense demands you check to see if that is the case in reality. Participants in *The City of Forking Paths* thus became entangled in a complex meshwork of virtual and physical reality, where video sequences pushed human behaviours into challenging perceptual territory. This is smartphone–spacetime as a vector for emergence in mobile art, where the participant and phone occupy a unique locus of points and expressions. Here, the phone operates like a portal—in the concrete physical sense that the device became a door—whose precise movement in conjunction with the body articulated an open-ended architectonic that algorithmically produced a series of surreal happenings on both sides (physical and virtual).

Engaging the cultural techniques instantiated by mobile devices, such a touch capacitance and geo-location, a participant who triggers a Cloud-based network to access art must also be considered as a co-composer of the artwork (Manning 2013). The process of exploring AR art goes beyond a user-centred experience, since the augments are only made visible by the participant triggering them by using a device. Until the augments are triggered, they remain on the network, yet have not emerged: they are part of a parallel reality that is virtual until actualised by the participant. Without the participant, there is no artwork. In this sense, they can be considered, with the artist, to co-compose the work. Conceptually, this idea is strongly related to theoretical concepts emerging from the posthuman digital humanities (Hayles 1999; Braidotti 2006, 2013), where technical devices are considered to extend, enhance and problematise the human body and its relation to culture and sociality. Braidotti (2013) argues that though cross-pollination, hybridisation and alternative theoretical modalities the humanities have become the "posthuman" digital humanities. A similar processual shift is occurring in the digital arts, where posthumanism comes increasingly into play.

For example, in *Biomer Skelters* (2013–), Thiel and Pappenheimer used the participant's physiological data—derived from a smartphone app attached to a Zephyr heart-rate monitor—to grow a virtual biome in physical space. Split into two teams—the "Indigenators" and the "Exoticators"—participants propagate either a biome of native plants or a biome of introduced species around their trajectory in real time, generated by an active yet calm heart rate. In tune with their environment as they walk, the new cartography emerges, driven by the relation between software, augments and the human body in urban space. Conceptually and pragmatically, the participant rather than the artist is the instantiator of the work: their performative actions are essential in propagating the biome that generates the artwork as an expressive algorithmic entity. Using techniques of décollage and assemblage, Tamiko Thiel and Will Pappenheimer consider their artwork to be a software assemblage (Wright 2015; Thiel and Pappenheimer 2016), that is, a "machinic assemblage" (Deleuze and Guatarri 1987) composed through the agential relations of software, code and algorithms. Considering such AR art as a software assemblage rather, than using the more conventional terms such as site-specific installation articulates a new materialist take on interfacing that emphasises such practices as participatory on the one hand and algorithmic on the other. In this process, where highly specific and differentiated meanings are traced by the participant), the idea emerges that the participant co-composes the artwork, triggered by contact with the virtual biome. Such gestures of co-composition move beyond the humanist model of art spectatorship. Taking a lead from Braidotti (2013), such artworks should be considered as posthuman digital arts, since they eschew the traditional models of humanist spectatorship—where the audience occupies a delimited role as the viewer of an artwork—in favour of an activated and embodied modality where affective computing sutures to sociality across a vibrant and emergent cartographies. In addition to the manifestly posthuman phenomena where smartphone and body move together across a shared topological space, smartphones are embedded in spacetime through their networked affordances.

John Craig Freeman's pioneering contribution to mobile AR art explores notions of portals, vectors, parallel worlds and simultaneous geographies. Freeman is currently one of the most prolific artists of the important ManifestAR group (Freeman 2012)—along with Will Pappenheimer and Tamiko Thiel—and co-authored their seminal manifesto of AR art (Freeman 2012). In the recent Los Angeles County Museum of Art (LACMA) iteration of *EEG AR: Things We Have Lost* (2015), Freeman posed a simple question to people on the streets of Los Angeles: "What have you lost?" The diverse responses of the people were then graphically represented (using the technique of photogrammetry) before being placed in AR and mapped as "points of interest" to the actual locations where the items were lost. Participants could then essentially "recover" their lost items using their smartphones, following the entire map if they wished to recover other participants' lost items as well. Covering a large section of Los Angeles, this "map of lost things" became a city walk, where Freeman performed guided tours during the course of the exhibition. In tandem with the walks, Freeman ran a medical "clinic" inside LACMA's Art + Technology Lab, where people were asked to don an EEG (electroencephalogram) machine and attempt to recover images of lost things from the graphical archive, using their brainwave patterns as triggers. Here, he drew on the methodology of electracy (Ulmer 2002) and the cultural technique of "choramancy", developed during his collaborative practice with eminent theorist Gregory Ulmer (Ulmer and Freeman 2014).

Freeman's work explores the potential for networked art to reclaim the civic space of cities as interactive and expressive spaces and draws on Gregory Ulmer's concept of electracy to develop an understanding of the role of the activist-artist in reclaiming urban space as their own, rather than the more prevalent conception of public space as either the property of corporate or government interests. Freeman comments of his geo-located AR art:

The act of navigating a space by following virtual objects is reminiscent of the Situationist dérive. Travel and mobility are key to art that relies on this dérive, the experience of walking, of encountering place. The virtual objects and their placement at specific GPS coordinates are not unlike the *plateau tourné*. (2015, p. 69)

In creating an alternative cartography based on a dérive where the public can "encounter place" Freeman articulates a desire to explore the potential of AR as a new modality of urban experience. In *Portal to an Alternative Reality* (2016), people were invited to enter a metaphoric portal, placed in a busy street in Hong Kong. Here, participants did not simply "view" the artwork. Rather, they were part of an encounter with another reality: a portal assembled from 3D images using incredibly life-like photogrammetry techniques, geo-located at a popular public location in Tsim Sha Tsui, Hong Kong (Fig. 12.1). AR as art practice leverages geo-location coupled with digital imaging to produce new cartographies that initiate a reconsideration of the material relations

Fig. 12.1   John Craig Freeman's *Portal to an Alternative Reality*, Hong Kong, commissioned by the Zero1 American Arts Incubator and the 22nd International Symposium on Electronic Art. Image used with kind permission of the artist

between technological networks (such as the Cloud), human experience and social affects as they coalesce in an activated urban ecology. Tamiko Thiel's community-based advisory practice focusses on interactions between marginalised communities and public space. Produced by the Caribbean Cultural Centre and African Diaspora Institute in East Harlem, Thiel trained members of the East Harlem community to use AR, and assisted with placing augments through geo-location at the sites in their community they felt were appropriate. In this work, the embodied and embedded knowledge of people from the community was mapped back to the landscape as digital manifestations of their dreams, desires and hopes for the future of East Harlem.

Mi Querido Barrio reveals the capacity of AR art to relay knowledge systems back to the actual physical sites that knowledge is drawn from, allowing technical networks to function as a relational force for communal change. Artistic projects that engage digital activism, connect up with the posthuman digital humanities project of understanding the negative effects of advanced capitalism, across diverse global strata and with recourse given to cultural specificity and respect for minority communities. The "makers" of the work—the community members Thiel trained in AR art—were able to create previously unreferenced cartographies that spoke to their specific cultural take on East Harlem, from a personal and political perspective. From the subject position of maker, they are able to generate meanings that speak to their relational and embodied experience of the city, mapping those meanings back to the urban landscape itself via the process of augmentation.

BIBLIOGRAPHY

Berry, M., & Schleser, M. (Eds.). (2014). *Mobile media making in an age of smartphones*. New York: Springer.
Braidotti, R. (2006). Posthuman, all too human: Towards a new process ontology. *Theory, Culture & Society, 23*(7–8), 197–208.
Braidotti, R. (2013). *The posthuman*. Oxford: Polity Press.
Deleuze, G., & Guattari, F. (1987). *A thousand plateaus: Capitalism and schizophrenia* (B. Massumi, Trans.). Minnesota: University of Minnesota Press.
Einstein, A. (1905). On the electrodynamics of moving bodies. *The principle of relativity*. London: Methuen and Company Ltd.
Freeman, J. C. (2012, February). ManifestAR: An augmented reality manifesto. In *IS&T/SPIE electronic imaging* (pp. 82890D–82890D). Bellingham, WA: International Society for Optics and Photonics.

Freeman, J. C. (2015). Emergent technology as art practice and public art as intervention. In *L.A.Re.Play: Mobile network culture in placemaking*. Leonardo Electronic Almanac, Volume 21, Number 1.

Geroimenko, V. (Ed.) (2018). *Augmented reality art: From an emerging technology to a novel creative medium* (2nd ed.). Cham: Springer.

Hayles, K. (1999). *How we became posthuman: Virtual bodies in cybernetics, literature, and informatics*. Chicago, IL: University of Chicago Press.

Manning, E. (2013). *Always more than one: Individuation's dance*. Durham: Duke University Press.

Thiel, T., & Pappenheimer, W. (2016). Assemblage and décollage in virtual public space. *Media-N: The Journal of the New Media Caucus*.

Ulmer, G. L. (2002). *Internet invention: From literacy to electracy*. New York: Longman.

Ulmer, G. L., & Freeman, J. C. (2014). Beyond the virtual public square: Ubiquitous computing and the new politics of well-being. In V. Geroimenko (Ed.), *Augmented reality art* (pp. 61–79). Cham: Springer.

Wright, R. (2014a). From the bleeding edge of the network: Augmented reality and the 'software assemblage'. In H. Ferreira & A. Vicente (Eds.), *Post screen: Device, medium and concept*. Lisbon: CIEBA-FBAUL.

Wright, R. (2014b). Art, in your pocket: New currents in mobile augmented reality. *Journal of Creative Technologies, 4*(MINA Special Issue), 1–8, 11.

Wright, R. (2015). Mobile augmented reality art and the politics of re-assembly. In *Proceedings of the 21st International Symposium on Electronic Art ISEA2015 Vancouver*. Retrieved from http://isea2015.org/publications/proceedings-of-the-21st-international-symposium-on-electronic-art/.

Wright, R. (2016). Augmented reality as experimental art practice: From information overlay to software assemblage. In *Proceedings of the 22nd International Symposium on Electronic Art ISEA2016 Hong Kong*. Retrieved from https://isea2016.scm.cityu.edu.hk/openconf/modules/request.php?-module=oc_program&action=view.php&id=135&type=4&a=.

Artworks and Apps. Cited

Cardiff, J., & Bures Miller, G. (2014). *The City of Forking Paths*. Augmented reality app. Geo-fenced to The Rocks, Sydney, Australia. Retrieved from https://itunes.apple.com/us/app/the-city-of-forking-paths/id870332593?mt=8. Walk duration, 66 mins.

Freeman, J. C. (2013–ongoing). *Things we have lost: EEG AR*, artwork was performed as iterations at FACT Gallery (Liverpool 2013), Los Angeles County Museum of Art (California 2015), and Coimbra, (Portugal 2014) https://johncraigfreeman.wordpress.com/ and http://www.lacma.org/eeg-ar-things-we-have-lost.

Freeman, J. C. (2016). Portal to an alternative reality. In *22nd International Symposium on Electronic Art ISEA2016 Hong Kong and Zero1Arts Incubator*, Wuhan, China.

Thiel, T. (2016). *Mi Querido Barrio* [My Beloved Community]. Augmented reality walk made with members of the Puerto Rican Community, presented by the Caribbean Cultural Centre African Diaspora Institute (http://www. cccadi.org), East Harlem, New York, USA.

Thiel, T., & Pappenheimer, W. (2013–ongoing). *Biomer Skelters*. Augmented reality app. Available in various locations, dimensions variable. Retrieved from https://www.layar.com/layers/biomerskelters.

PART III

Making Change

CHAPTER 13

Siyashuta! Capturing Police Brutality on Mobile Phones in South Africa

Lorenzo Dalvit and Alette Schoon

Abstract Many poor Black South Africans are starting to find their voice by capturing events on mobile phone cameras, ubiquitous devices amongst all sectors of society. Citizens' video journalism is providing visual evidence that cannot be mollified by political rhetoric, exposing injustices such as illegal corporal punishment at schools, gang rape and police violence. These mobile videos, through the platform of a tabloid newspaper's Facebook page, function as catalysts that allow narratives of critique to emerge and grow through social media conversations.

Keywords Mobile journalism · South Africa · Online videos

Two decades after the end of Apartheid, South Africa remains a deeply divided and largely unequal society. The increasing gap between rich and poor is manifest in all aspects of society, including the media, which predominantly promotes the voice of the middle class and the powerful (Friedman 2011). Tabloids such as the *Daily Sun*, targeting a growing

L. Dalvit · A. Schoon (✉)
School of Journalism and Media Studies, Rhodes University,
Grahamstown, South Africa

© The Author(s) 2018
M. Schleser and M. Berry (eds.), *Mobile Story Making in an Age of Smartphones*, https://doi.org/10.1007/978-3-319-76795-6_13

African readership, are a particularly interesting phenomenon in this respect as they pose a potential challenge to mainstream media through highlighting issues important to the poor (Wasserman 2013). These tabloids can provide a platform for citizen journalism produced on mobile phones.

More than 70% of the poorest South Africans were in possession of mobile phones during the period that the mobile media featured in this study was produced, and more than a third of such phones could access the mobile internet (Gillwald et al. 2012). Banda (2010) has argued that citizen journalism could play an important role in Africa given the extreme inequalities that plague the continent and that mobile phones are central to such journalism due to the technology's ubiquity on the continent. Despite examples from other countries, research on the role of citizen journalists' mobile phone videos in reporting crime and ensuring accountability in South Africa is still emerging.

CONTEXT

Bruce (2002) notes the need to interrogate the link between the repressive role of the South African police under Apartheid and police brutality since 1994. A decade after the video screenings of police violence against migrants that open Bruce's report, the issues of police brutality and its coverage by the media are brought back into public discussion by incidents such as the death of activist Andries Tatane and by the shooting of protesting miners at the Marikana mine (see Wasserman 2013). In both cases, professional journalists were behind the camera, but members of poor communities are increasingly using mobile phones to video abuse.

The *Daily Sun* actively engages readers to submit such videos to their journalists through Bluetooth. Unlike most broadsheet newspapers, its journalists live in the communities they report on. In many of the videos, the person filming can be heard saying "I am taking this to the *Daily Sun*", illustrating how the tabloid is imagined as a tool for social justice. In response to the paper's lack of credibility with mainstream journalists, who dismiss the tabloid for its focus on witchcraft (see Steenveld and Strelitz 2010), the video editor emphasises its people-centered approach. The focus is on getting the story out quickly, instead of spending a lot of time in finding out whether stories are indeed true, but visitors who were present are invited to comment. Thus, like many tabloid newspapers, the *Daily Sun* can be considered a "producerly text" (Fiske 2002, p. 76), in that it allows readers to assist in producing meaning and contested interpretations, and substitutes the rational unified truth of the middle-class public sphere with what can be called "the melodramatic imagination" (Steenveld and Strelitz 2010). In Africa, the oppositional tools of the dispossessed to counter the despot are not rational debate, but instead operates in the dubious realm of rumour (Mbembe 2001). The power of pavement gossip and rumour to challenge mainstream media is encapsulated in the West African phrase "radio trottoir" (Ellis 1989). This avoidance of the unified rational narrative of the public sphere needs to be understood in terms of the difficulty of the subaltern subject to claim a unified voice, given the dispossession of any notion of subaltern subjecthood in (post)colonial discourse (Spivak 1988). One may therefore understand the nature of the media of the marginalised to be fragmented and lacking in unified narrative and truth.

New media, with its instant access to many voices, and through its ubiquity and interactivity (Lievrouw and Livingstone 2006), becomes a powerful tool in producing narratives from such fragments. Due to the ubiquity of mobile phones, schoolchildren can now film their teacher exerting, for instance, illegal corporal punishment and send it to the *Daily Sun*. Interactivity allows ordinary people to participate in such acts as identifying the security guards who savagely beat an old lady for shoplifting, so that *Daily Sun* readers could gather enough evidence to open a case and convict the guards for assault. Users of the *Daily Sun*'s Facebook page frequently request that copies of these videos be sent to them via WhatsApp so they can share them with friends in separate offline spaces of rumour through mobile media circulation or a "pavement internet" (Walton 2014). Through the public platform of comments on its Facebook page, the *Daily Sun* is arguably able to create a form of national public sphere for its readers. Here, they can collectively start to make sense of these videos, melodramatic fragments of stories of people like themselves, even though this is not the rational Habermasian public sphere of mainstream media. The *Daily Sun*'s video editor engages in several strategies to make the videos more cohesive, such as adding subtitles to contextualise the action as well as cutting for length to minimise download time and prioritise action. Videos are uploaded to the *Daily Sun*'s Facebook page, which most visitors (80%) access via a mobile phone.

METHOD

We consider videos covering three events published on the *Daily Sun*'s Facebook page between January 2012 and October 2013. Our concern is specifically with videos on police brutality. The recent sentencing of the policemen in one of the videos as well as the protests against police violence in the United States give this topic currency and global resonance. We have selected videos filmed by readers and thus did not analyse videos by *Daily Sun* reporters. There are other citizen journalism videos on the site that deal with violence, but these are between ordinary people inside the community. Firstly, we analyse the tentative narratives that emerge in the spectacular violent excess of the videos themselves, and then we consider how these very subjective experiences are analysed and given meaning through Facebook comments. The comments by Facebook users on these videos are subjected to a qualitative thematic content analysis (Snelson 2016). The purpose of the analysis is to show the systemic nature of police brutality by foregrounding shared experiences.

ANALYSIS

The first video in our analysis is titled "Mpumalanga traffic cops attack a funeral undertaker driver". The video itself is not particularly dramatic. It starts with an image of a group of men in brown uniform, the traffic police, crowding over a body lying on the gravel road. Subtitles reveal that this person is a funeral undertaker who was assaulted by traffic police after he refused to pay a bribe when he was found parking illegally. The angle of the camera is slightly off kilter and at a distance, suggesting a cautious non-professional filmmaker. Nevertheless, we hear the person filming the scene saying "Ndimelanga *Daily Sun*" (I will send this to the *Daily Sun*), a threat that is not taken very seriously by the traffic police, who continue struggling to lift the person up from the ground. The camera pans to the right to reveal that the videographer is standing behind three other onlookers, who are shielding him from the view of the traffic cops. Then we see a wide shot of the three traffic cops pushing the semi-conscious man into the back of the vehicle. The subtitles reveal that the person filming is the undertaker's colleague. While the subtitles are undoubtedly central to making sense of the story, its authority stems from the positionality it provides the viewer—as seeing through the eyes of the undertaker's colleague.

Subjective storytelling is a characteristic of mobile video, created through the personal and intimate nature of the media device (Schleser 2014). In the case of the undertaker's colleague, this subjectivity becomes the subjectivity of erasure, characteristic of powerless blackness (Mbembe 2001; Fanon 2008). The colleague is ignored by the traffic police, even when he states that he is filming, his lack of agency otherwise portrayed by his distance from the scene and positioning himself behind others. It is only through the assertion of the name of the newspaper and through his mobile camera that he can claim any power. Internationally, storytelling in video journalism is commonly produced either through the diegetic narration of professional video journalists or citizen video journalists who tell stories through juxtaposing interviews with ordinary people on the scene (Bock 2012). In these videos, however, stories are told not primarily through words but through the direct experience of seeing a moment of transgression, a rupture of the illusion of a society based on human rights, through the eyes of the filmmaker. Watching such a film becomes a corporeal experience, as mobile video spectatorship often suggests various relationships between the body and the screen and the face and the screen (Richardson 2010).

This corporeal spectatorship is even more apparent in the next video. Entitled "Police Brutality", the subtitles reveal that this is Phase 9 Mangaung in the Free State, and the scene seems to be a building site. The video at first appears objective: an invisible filmmaker tracks an apprehended man who is being followed by two police officers who repeatedly hit him on the head with a baton. The subtitles reveal that a member of the public caught this brutality on video. The video's focus shifts quickly to the filmmaker. One of the police officers looks up into the lens of the camera and in a moment of recognition of the filming runs towards the camera, shouting. The camera shakes. The subtitles indicate: "The cops then attacked him, damaging his one ear." We see a sliver of the building site through the darkness of the hand that clasps the phone to protect it. No questions are asked. The moment of the policeman's shift in gaze thus creates a relationship between the screen and the imagined body of the filmmaker, as the image is suddenly embodied, and police brutality witnessed through the vulnerability of both this body as well as the body of the phone. Bock (2012) argues that the citizen journalist lacks institutional power and has limited authority, an authority expressed through linguistic skill and charisma.

Here, however, the filmmaker's authority lies in his body. Perceiving the world through the eyes of someone who can be attacked with impunity, who does not even feel able to argue back to injustice, makes the erasure of the black subject visible. A narrative of survival is transformed into one of injustice through the spectator realising a shared subjectivity with the filmmaker. In the Facebook comments for this story, two remarks stand out. These are narratives of when police assumed they were dealing with a powerless, marginalised black person—the unemployed that under neoliberalism have come to be regarded as "waste" (Mbembe 2001)—only to discover that the person was a soldier, or a lawyer. Such comments highlight how human rights are often reserved for those who have employment.

The final two videos offer two perspectives on a brutal event in which police abused and tortured Mozambican national Mido Macia. Like the undertaker in the second video, Macia, a taxi driver, refused to pay a bribe for illegal parking. These videos contain no subtitles, only the shouting of the crowd. In "Killer cops caught on video", a police officer in a bulletproof vest is confronting Macia, who has his back to the camera. Another police officer appears behind the car and they shove him to one side while our citizen journalist's edges closer, his or her finger in front of the lens, enabling a subjective awareness. Three other police officers arrive to help while the crowd starts to shout swearwords. One person yells to those who are filming "Shuta, shuta nanku!" (Shoot, shoot the other side!) The citizen journalist struggles to get an angle on Macia and then reveals that the man is now on the ground, his hands tied to the police van, which then commences to drag him behind the accelerating van. We hear people in the crowd alternatively shouting "Suka wena" (Fuck off) and "Siyashuta!" (We are shooting you). For a moment, another screen on a BlackBerry phone enters the frame of our video, revealing how many in the crowd are responding to the injustice through mobile photography. We hear a man's voice shout, incredulously, "Hayibo!" (That's crazy!). This video went viral very quickly, leading to police responding that their response was justified as Macia raised a gun during the altercation. However, due to the ubiquity of the mobile phone, another video could quickly dispel this allegation. A second video was also posted by the *Daily Sun* under the title "Killer cops: new video shows police version is NOT true" and was instrumental to disputing the police version and showing that Macia never assaulted an officer. These videos attracted more than 1000 comments on the

Daily Sun Facebook page, as readers debated whether these police officers were typical or simply "bad apples". Nearly 500 condemned the act. Many shared their experiences of injustice with the police and there were calls for burning down police stations and even killing police officers. Several people represented this police brutality as a continuation of Apartheid brutality. Thulani Xola's comment is telling in that he uses metaphors that show a lack of human recognition as he laments how police are "killing people in SA like flies" and refers to the recent police "slaughtering" of Marikana mineworkers.[1] Another commentator, Jimmy Ndlovu, complains that police officers are above the law: "All we can do is take photos and videos then post'em on social networks."

Conclusion

Taken not as isolated cases, but as examples of systemic violence, these videos challenge the mainstream media's narrative of transformation. They do so not through cohesive narratives, but through a corporeal form of witnessing of brutality, an extreme form of spectacular subjectivity.

However, while the mainstream media treats such violence as isolated incidents, the online discussion on these pages reveals the shared experience of such violence amongst poor South Africans who have to subsist outside a rights culture. Despite giving voice to such concerns, the *Daily Sun*, however, does not attempt an analysis or commentary that may highlight the systemic inequalities of South African society, but instead simply focuses on the spectacular and sensationalist aspects of the images.

Note

1. All Facebook commentators have been allocated pseudonyms.

Appendix: Videos from the *Daily Sun*'s Website

Grade 10 pupil being beaten by teacher, http://www.youtube.com/watch?v=bZoQvx2q-Uo.

Granny accused of theft is beaten up, http://www.youtube.com/watch?v=05cM69jfvTM.

Killer cops caught on video, http://www.youtube.com/watch?v=xnLNX_Ux7J4.

Killer cops—new video, http://www.youtube.com/watch?v=eMRBtlCYobU.
Mpumalanga traffic cops attack a funeral undertaker driver, http://www.
youtube.com/watch?v=Kkg3_0Jsto0.
Police brutality in South Africa, http://www.youtube.com/watch?v=
S6-EVRLuUwo.

BIBLIOGRAPHY

Banda, F. (2010). *Citizen journalism & democracy in Africa: An exploratory study*. Grahamstown, South Africa: Highway Africa.
Bock, M. A. (2012). Citizen video journalists and authority in narrative: Reviving the role of the witness. *Journalism, 13*(5), 639–653.
Bruce, D. (2002). *Police brutality in South Africa*. Inter-African Network for Human Rights and Development (Afronet).
Ellis, S. (1989). Tuning into pavement radio. *African Affairs, 88*(352), 321–330.
Fanon, F. (2008). *Black skin, white masks* (New ed.). London: Pluto-Press.
Fiske, J. (2002). *Television culture*. London and New York: Routledge.
Friedman, S. (2011). Whose freedom? South Africa's press, middle-class bias and the threat of control. *Ecquid Novi: African Journalism Studies, 32*(2), 106–121.
Gillwald, A., Moyo, M., & Stork, C. (2012). *Understanding what is happening in ICT in South Africa: A supply- and demand-side analysis of the ICT sector* (Policy Paper No. 7). Cape Town, South Africa: Research ICT Africa.
Lievrouw, L., & Livingstone, S. (2006). The social shaping and consequences of ICTs. In L. Lievrouw & S. Livingstone (Eds.), *Handbook of new media: Social shaping and social consequences of ICTs* (pp. 15–30). Los Angeles: Sage.
Mbembe, A. (2001). *On the postcolony*. Berkeley: University of California Press.
Richardson, I. (2010). Faces, interfaces, screens: Relational ontologies of framing, attention and distraction. *Transformations, 18*.
Schleser, M. (2014). Connecting through mobile autobiographies: Self-reflexive mobile filmmaking, self-representation, and selfies. In *Mobile media making in an age of smartphones* (pp. 148–158). New York: Palgrave.
Snelson, C. L. (2016). Qualitative and mixed methods social media research: A review of the literature. *International Journal of Qualitative Methods, 15*(1). https://doi.org/10.1177/1609406915624574.
Spivak, G. C. (1988). Can the subaltern speak? In C. Nelson & L. Grossberg (Eds.), *Marxism and the interpretation of culture* (pp. 271–313). Champaign, IL: University of Illinois Press.

Steenveld, L., & Strelitz, L. (2010). Trash or popular journalism? The case of South Africa's Daily Sun. *Journalism: Theory, Practice & Criticism, 11*(5), 531–547.

Walton, M. (2014). Pavement internet: Mobile media economies and ecologies for young people in South Africa. In G. Goggin & L. Hjorth (Eds.), *The routledge companion to mobile media* (pp. 450–461). London: Routledge.

Wasserman, H. (2013). Journalism in a new democracy: The ethics of listening. *Communicatio, 39*(1), 67–84.

CHAPTER 14

Devising Mobile Apps: Participatory Design for Endemic Diseases Transmitted by the Mosquito *Aedes* (Dengue, Zika and Chikungunya)

Tiago Franklin Rodrigues Lucena, Ana Paula Machado Velho, Vinicius Durval Dorne and Diana Maria Gallicchio Domingues

Abstract Dengue, zika and chikungunya are endemic diseases transmitted by *Aedes aegypti* mosquitoes that are affecting different countries in the world. Current efforts to control the mosquito are more

T. F. R. Lucena (✉)
Health Promotion Graduate Program, UniCesumar and ICETI-Cesumar
Institute of Science, Technology, and Innovation, Paraná, Brazil

A. P. M. Velho
State University of Maringá, Paraná, Brazil

V. D. Dorne
Federal University of Uberlandia, Minas Gerais, Brazil

D. M. G. Domingues
Biomedical Engineering Graduate Program, Gama–Unb and Science
and Health Technologies Graduate Program, Ceilandia, Brazil

© The Author(s) 2018
M. Schleser and M. Berry (eds.), *Mobile Story Making in an Age of Smartphones*, https://doi.org/10.1007/978-3-319-76795-6_14

139

effective when combined with the collaboration of population. Efforts to limit the number of cases have not been sufficiently effective and community engagement is essential to control the number of mosquitoes in the environment. This chapter describes the process of development of mobile apps designed to promote health and combat *Aedes*. The strategy was to engage the community and students from different levels in a city in of Brazil to devise, in a participatory design approach, apps to "fight" *Aedes*.

Keywords Mobile apps · Participatory design · Community engagement

Dengue, zika and chikungunya are diseases transmitted by *Aedes aegypti* mosquitoes that are affecting Brazil and other countries around the world. Current efforts to control the mosquito combine chemical and biological strategies and the management of breeding sites (World Health Organization 2009). Researchers have also highlighted the importance of engaging the population for vector control in their domiciliary areas (Pérez et al. 2007).

In order to devise some possibilities, we engaged the community and students in a city in the south of Brazil to work together and design new perspectives to deal with these diseases. We used a participatory design approach (Sjöberg and Timpka 1998) and, as a result, the community we worked with came up with mobile apps as an idea to create better tools to combat *Aedes*. Smartphones can help to track and predict diseases in real time (Waegemann 2010) and are a promising approach in monitoring the outbreaks, such as the cases of malaria in Kenya described by Wesolwski et al. (2012). This new approach of collecting epidemiological data with the collaboration of the community has been called participatory epidemiology (Freifeld et al. 2010). Collecting data from the population using smartphones has also been used to gain an understanding of disease transmission (Santosh Vijaykumar et al. 2016).

After our health intervention, supported by a community-based participatory research (Israel et al. 1998), twenty-four apps were sketched and one prototyped in order to support users in sharing their stories about the disease using smartphones and to reveal breeding sites to public agencies. This chapter describes the artistic, communication and design background of this creative process, which brings together mobile technologies, community participation and health promotion.

PARTICIPATORY DESIGN: MOBILE APPS AS A TOOL TO COMBAT *AEDES*

Besides the official data about dengue, zika and chikungunya, there are still many unreported cases (WHO 2016). These endemic diseases require an interdisciplinary and *bio-eco-social* approach (Quintero et al. 2014) and, according to the National Dengue Control Plan (NDCP), one of ten components and strategies listed to combat *Aedes* is encouraging community collaboration to reduce breeding sites.

Interventions to control *Aedes* based on the participation of the community, when combined with other actions, can improve the efficiency of the prevention (Heintze et al. 2007). Over the last three years we have been promoting strategies to engage people in the Borba Gato district in Maringá to create stories about their experience with the environment.[1] "*Mutirões*"—collective acts to walk through the streets to pick up litter— were organised by the communities. Cooperation is also required when community health agents visit houses to check if there are breeding sites. These agents can also perceive whether there have been advances in people's actions towards improvement of the environment.

Sharing stories online takes advantage of the pervasive and ubiquitous presence of connected devices around the world. Unlike other projects that have created apps to support data collection by health agents in the field (designed by specialists, and to be used by them), such as that proposed by Lwin et al. (2016), we invited the community into the process of creation and design and to think up, from the outset, new approaches to combat *Aedes* using smartphones.

By taking a participatory approach, we mean research that engages people usually regarded as "subjects" in "aspects of research design and/or process (participatory), with an explicit intention of generating practical changes (action)" (Banks et al. 2013). We emphasise that the production of stories about the disease is an important factor to create empathy between individuals inside the community. Studies also confirmed that when a local newspaper brings a narrative and a voice of a neighbour into the news, this person might be more effective in the mobilisation and empowerment of the community (Shen et al. 2014).

The growing use of *participatory epidemiology* terminology is an example of a bottom-up perspective: researchers acquire data from the population (especially in social networks) in order to predict, act or understand their opinion about some disease (Freifeld et al. 2010; Seltzer et al. 2015; Southwell et al. 2016). Recently, researchers also have been using internet-based disease monitoring tools such as "engine query data" (Ginsberg et al. 2009; Gluskin et al. 2014), Twitter activity to track levels of H1N1 pandemic (Signorini et al. 2011) and opinions about public health campaigns (Harris et al. 2014; Seltzer et al. 2015).

CREATION METHODOLOGY

This work is based on collaborative practices involving artists, journalists, students and inhabitants of the Borba Gato district. Our approach with the community has previously been discussed (Velho et al. 2016); on this occasion we collected multimedia content (videos, photos, sketches, drawings and texts) produced by the community after our intervention about their experiences about *Aedes*. Interviews with members of the community who suffered from *Aedes* were full of emotional expressions such as "take care", "felt bad", "my son got sick and we suffered", "we felt terrible". These stories were uploaded using mobile phones to groups created on Facebook and WhatsApp. Some of this content was analysed and used by young journalists from our group in their reports, enabling them to produce news not based solely on official data provided by health agencies. The rich content produced autonomously by the community guided the academic reflection of the students on the postgraduate programme of Health Promotion and Clean Technologies at UniCesumar.

In a second phase, and for the purpose of devising mobile apps, we invited participation from students on undergraduate and postgraduate courses at one public and one private institution. The different levels of collaboration between lower secondary school and sixth form students working together with undergraduate and postgraduate students and the community are shown in Fig. 14.1.

The structure of mobile apps was part of the students' assessment and they needed to relate their creation with locative and mobile technology topics in order to be graded. By developing apps, students were able to understand their roles as citizens and use their creativity in a socially engaged project. The direction of this project was to use games and

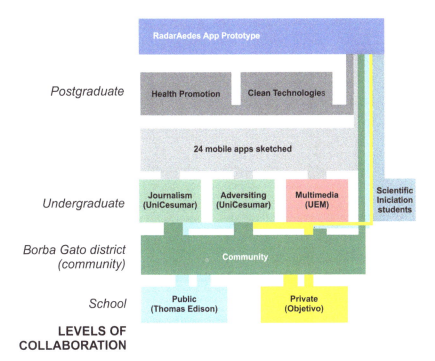

Fig. 14.1 Architecture of the participatory design: Engaging community and students to devise mobile apps to combat *Aedes*

mobilisation strategies to devise an mHealth app to combat *Aedes* and listen to the community and learn with them to propose the tools and functionalities.

Summarising initiatives of different projects, we prototyped a mobile app called "Radar*Aedes*", and the requirements and scopes of the system were designed after the intervention with an intense collaboration between the community and students (Ferreira et al. 2015).

RESULTS

Twenty-four mobile apps were purposed by different groups of students divided between public and private institutions. The names of these apps, their visual identity and architecture of information, navigation flows, wireframes and layouts were considered to be a part of the creative work and the grading system took the whole process into consideration. Table 14.1 shows the names and descriptions of twelve of the apps.

"Radar*Aedes* app", the final prototyped app, was made after an evaluation of the twenty-four apps presented. It was programed in Java (JPA RESTful) as back-end, following the good practices of Object-Oriented Programming (OOP), with REST architecture for front-end data integration. We used a MySQL relational database. As a standard to the graphic interface, we applied Ionic (Angularjs), based on material design guidelines for Google Android, following the good practices of user experience (UX) and user interface (UI). The code of the app was typed on Sublime Text, Notepad++ and String Tool Suite IDE (integrated developmentenvironment).

Besides the graphic interface, which needs improvement, the major contribution of the app was the possibility of giving the community tools for creation. The app has two functionalities that were highlighted by members of community: (1) breeding sites surveillance—people want to share photos of and information about places where the mosquito might be present (anonymously); and (2) a communication tool to organise group efforts to clean streets and abandoned areas.

The initial version of the app records the content and geo-locates it. Videos, images and texts can now be seen by other users online who can, for example, see geo-tagged images of dengue breeding sites to predictive surveillance. The possibility of geo-locating images as an important tool for reporting, as well as the security of information and levels of access, was also presented in many of the mobile apps devised. People who suspected that their neighbour was not "taking care" of the environment and wanted to send them an anonymous message could do so, as this aspect was listed as a relevant functionality for the app. This approach showed that members of community wanted to collaborate with public agencies by collecting and sharing images of breeding sites, so the app could be an interface between citizens and health authorities. Some of them wanted to receive "points" or discounts in public taxes.

In fact, this form of social participation has challenged governments, politicians, educators and health professionals. The growing use of social networks for civic participation has received more attention since Arab Spring movements confirmed the potential of the use of mobile technologies in civic actions (Castells 2012; Rheingold 2003). Over the past years, social mobilisation has also been a theme for many artists (Weibel 2015).

Table 14.1 List of twelve apps designed and their approach to combating *Aedes*

App	Description	Technological and creative approach
TOF -Tira o Foco (Get rid of the focus)	Online Social Network app with the aim of inviting a friend to help "clean" the environment. For this supportive help the "friend" can receive bonus points	• A tool to organize a group effort by location (street or district);
DenguInga	Location-based game app to manage competition between neighbourhoods. For each district a group is formed and headed by students. Public agencies can share numbers for each case in the districts and also give "missions" that can be accepted by groups	• Location-based game based on public data of the most affected places • Groups are also invited to help other districts and receive extra points when this information is confirmed
Não deixe água parada! (Don't leave still water)	Community event in the most affected district Music, dance and cultural shows with the theme of *Aedes* transmitted diseases	• Public event in neighbourhood where number of cases dropped • Bringing cultural events to the district is a way for the population to manifest themselves about their condition
RadarAedes	Reporting app. Neighbours are invited to take pictures with the location of a suspected focus and the data is shared with the sanitary agents; When it is confirmed the users who reported it receive points or a discount on public taxes	• Location-based pictures taken by users to support public agencies • Active users, confident about the true information can receive a discount on public taxes
AedesTeAchei (I've found you Aedes)	A game for kids—taking care of a virtual backyard	A literacy game tool to teach kids about breeding sites and how frequently they have to check the objects in the backyard
DengueSquad	A tool to organize group efforts and volunteers; People create an account with their profile; Using the app you can set up a group with certain objectives	• A group effort tool and an online social network for volunteers • points can be earned as you participate in a group effort and can be exchanged for products in local markets

(continued)

Table 14.1   (continued)

App	Description	Technological and creative approach
Aedes Checker	A multipurpose app—to report suspected breeding sites to public agencies	A tool for reporting—Health units geo-located, together with a list of symptoms of the disease (so that the user knows where to go if he suspects he has contracted it) Telemedicine communication tool with the health unit
Aedes Augmented	A data visualization tool— visualization of health data about *Aedes*-related diseases by location	A augment reality tool to visualize data about dengue based on health reports. Users can visualise synthetic "big mosquitoes" flying over the most affected areas. The size of the mosquito flying in the district is related to the number of suspected cases
Onde Esta *Aedes*? (Where's *Aedes*?)	A game with scenarios (based on pictures sent by users) to list	A game to identify breeding sites and most common objects where mosquitoes deposit eggs (different scenarios)
Aedes Report	A notification tool connected with official data of cases and also local news reports about *Aedes* disease cases in the city	Notification tool based on official data about *Aedes* diseases in each localities and challenges for each community

We situated our socially engaged approach with this background by allowing people to share their narratives about the disease and by inviting them to collaborate in a design process to create new strategies to combat *Aedes*.

CONCLUSION

The twenty-four layouts presented different approaches to combating *Aedes*, with many of them not listed in the literature. This is an example of how we can bring a community to the centre of a design process and, through this, we can participate in their intimate space and understand their concerns. More than 80% of apps highlight the smartphone as a communication tool (to report, to document and to organise people). People also understood that mobile media can be useful in mobilising their community. A prototype of one app, Radar*Aedes*, was created. The central concern was not so much to prove its efficiency: rather, it was using the process of designing *itself* as a way to think about our environment and its challenges.

The engagement of the population to support the project was influenced by the perspective that they were able to contribute to an innovative app based on their experiences in the environment. Many members of the community, including elderly, were curious about how their stories could be incorporated as a tool in an app.

The creative intervention opened up the possibility of a bottom-up approach to combat *Aedes*. It is clear that community participation is essential to reduce the vectors. Traditional educational strategies and mass media campaigns increase knowledge of the disease, but they are not crucial in changing behaviour. Inspiring the community to understand that they are actors for health promotion (not just the private sector and government) is essential to empowering them. The seasonality of the disease makes the evaluation of the health programmes hard, and ongoing. Integrated acts (official, public, communitarian, isolated) must be constant. Bringing the community to the centre of mobile media-making was an opportunity to promote a healthier environment and boost wellbeing and welfare.

Acknowledgements Ana P.M. Velho was funded by the National Council for Scientific and Technological Development post-doctorate scholarship project under the supervision of Diana Domingues (CNPq-PQ-1A). In addition, to Ted Krueger for valuable guidance and some refreshing ideas.

NOTE

1. Borba Gato is a district with some stigma in Maringá and its socio-spatial configuration may differ from other high-class planned districts in the city. The LIR*Aa* report points out that garbage and other waste remains are the main mosquito breeding sites (63.2%) of the total focal points, especially in Maringá. Among the main breeding sites, we are able to list potted plants, water tanks, drums, bowls and pots. According to LIR*Aa*, if people took care of the garbage and got rid of the saucers under the plant pots, 80% of outbreaks would be avoided. However, the vectors' ability to exploit unconventional sites to lay their eggs should not be underestimated (WHO | World Health Organization 2012).

BIBLIOGRAPHY

Banks, S., Armstrong, A., Carter, K., Graham, H., Hayward, P., Henry, A., et al. (2013). Everyday ethics in community-based participatory research. *Contemporary Social Science, 8*(3), 1–15. https://doi.org/10.1080/215820 41.2013.769618.

Castells, M. (2012). *Networks of outrage and hope: Social movements in the internet age* (1st ed.). Cambridge, UK: Polity.

Ferreira, A. C. R., Guilherme, Y., Velho, A. P. M., & Lucena, T. F. R. (2015). Aprimoramento do Conteúdo e Operacionalização do Aplicativo Radar Dengue: Uma experiência em Saúde e Tecnologia Móvel. *Anais Eletrônico: IX EPCC - Encontro Internacional de Produção Científica Unicesumar* (pp. 7–10). Unicesumar: Maringá-PR.

Freifeld, C. C., Chunara, R., Mekaru, S. R., Chan, E. H., Kass-Hout, T., Iacucci, A. A., et al. (2010). Participatory epidemiology: Use of mobile phones for community-based health reporting. *PLoS Medicine, 7*(12), 1–5. https://doi.org/10.1371/journal.pmed.1000376.

Ginsberg, J., Mohebbi, M. H., Patel, R. S., Brammer, L., Smolinski, M. S., & Brilliant, L. (2009). Detecting influenza epidemics using search engine query data. *Nature, 457*(7232), 1012–1014. https://doi.org/10.1038/nature07634.

Gluskin, R. T., Johansson, M. A., Santillana, M., & Brownstein, J. S. (2014). Evaluation of internet-based dengue query data: Google dengue trends. *PLoS Neglected Tropical Diseases, 8*(2), 1–6. https://doi.org/10.1371/journal.pntd.0002713.

Harris, J. K., Moreland-Russell, S., Choucair, B., Mansour, R., Staub, M., & Simmons, K. (2014). Tweeting for and against public health policy: Response to the Chicago Department of Public Health's electronic cigarette Twitter campaign. *Journal of Medical Internet Research, 16*(10), e238. https://doi.org/10.2196/jmir.3622.

Heintze, C., Garrido, M. V., & Kroeger, A. (2007). What do community-based dengue control programmes achieve? A systematic review of published evaluations. *Transactions of the Royal Society of Tropical Medicine and Hygiene, 101*(4), 317–325. https://doi.org/10.1016/j.trstmh.2006.08.007.

Israel, B. A., Schulz, A. J., Parker, E. A., & Becker, A. B. (1998). Review of community-based research: Assessing partnership approaches to improve public health. *Annual Review of Public Health, 19*, 173–202. https://doi.org/10.1146/annurev.publhealth.19.1.173.

Lwin, M. O., Vijaykumar, S., Rathnayake, V. S., Lim, G., Panchapakesan, C., Foo, S., et al. (2016). A social media mHealth solution to address the needs of dengue prevention and management in Sri Lanka. *Journal of Medical Internet Research, 18*(7), e149. https://doi.org/10.2196/jmir.4657.

Pérez, D., Lefèvre, P., Sánchez, L., Sánchez, L. M., Boelaert, M., Kourí, G., et al. (2007). Community participation in Aedes aegypti control: A sociological perspective on five years of research in the health area "26 de Julio", Havana, Cuba. *Tropical Medicine & International Health, 12*(5), 664–672. https://doi.org/10.1111/j.1365-3156.2007.01833.x.

Quintero, J., Brochero, H., Manrique-Saide, P., Barrera-Pérez, M., Basso, C., Romero, S., et al. (2014). Ecological, biological and social dimensions of dengue vector breeding in five urban settings of Latin America: A multi-country study. *BMC Infectious Diseases, 14*, 38. https://doi.org/10.1186/1471-2334-14-38.

Rheingold, H. (2003). *Smart mobs: The next social revolution*. New York: Basic Books.

Seltzer, E. K., Jean, N. S., Kramer-Golinkoff, E., Asch, D. A., & Merchant, R. M. (2015). The content of social media's shared images about Ebola: A retrospective study. *Public Health, 129*(9), 1273–1277. https://doi.org/10.1016/j.puhe.2015.07.025.

Shen, F., Ahern, L., & Baker, M. (2014). Stories that count: Influence of news narratives on issue attitudes. *Journalism & Mass Communication Quarterly, 91*(1), 98–117. https://doi.org/10.1177/1077699013514414.

Signorini, A., Segre, A. M., & Polgreen, P. M. (2011). The use of Twitter to track levels of disease activity and public concern in the U.S. during the influenza A H1N1 pandemic. *PLoS ONE, 6*(5). https://doi.org/10.1371/journal.pone.0019467.

Sjöberg, C., & Timpka, T. (1998). Participatory design of information systems in health care. *Journal of the American Medical Informatics Association, 5*(2), 177–183. https://doi.org/10.1136/jamia.1998.0050177.

Southwell, B. G., Dolina, S., Jimenez-Magdaleno, K., Squiers, L. B., & Kelly, B. J. (2016). Zika virus-related news coverage and online behavior, United States, Guatemala, and Brazil. *Emerging Infectious Diseases, 22*(7), 1320–1321. https://doi.org/10.3201/eid2207.160415.

Velho, A. P. M., Domingues, D., Lucena, T. F. R., & Dorne, V. D. (2016). 'Jornalismo etnográfico: um relato de mobilização contra a dengue (Ethnographic journalism: A dengue mobilization report)'. *Revista Brasileira de Ensino de Jornalismo, 6*(18), 121–136. Available at http://www.fnpj.org.br/rebej/ojs/index.php/rebej/article/view/426/282.

Vijaykumar, S., Lwin, M. O., Theng, Y.-L., Foo, S., Cheong, S. A., et al. (2016, February). A social media-based participatory epidemiology approach for vector-borne disease prevention (VBDP) in South Asia, *eTELEMED 2013: The Fifth International Conference on eHealth, Telemedicine and Social Medicine*, 194–197. https://dr.ntu.edu.sg/handle/10220/10053.

Waegemann, C. P. (2010). mHealth: The next generation of telemedicine? *Telemedicine and e-Health,* *16*(1), 23–25. https://doi.org/10.1089/tmj.2010.9990.

Weibel, P. (2015). *Global activism: Art and conflict in the 21st century.* Cambridge, MA: MIT Press.

Wesolowski, A., Eagle, N., Tatem, A. J., Smith, D. L., Noor, A. M., Snow, R. W., et al. (2012). Quantifying the impact of human mobility on malaria. *Science,* *338*(6104), 267–270. https://doi.org/10.1126/science.1223467.

World Health Organization. (2009). 'Dengue: Guidelines for diagnosis, treatment, prevention, and control'. *Special Programme for Research and Training in Tropical Diseases,* X, 147.

WHO | World Health Organization. (2012). *Global strategy for dengue prevention and control 2012–2020, World Health Organiszation, Geneva, Switzerland.* Geneva: WHO. Available at http://www.who.int/denguecontrol/9789241504034/en/.

WHO | World Health Organization. (2016). *Neglected tropical diseases, WHO.* World Health Organization. Available at http://www.who.int/neglected_diseases/diseases/en/ [accessed 10 November 2016].

CHAPTER 15

Mobile Framing: Vertical Videos from User-Generated Content to Corporate Marketing

Dave Neal and Miriam Ross

Abstract Although "vertical videos" have been derided as inelegant, amateur and to be avoided, a number of corporate organisations such as Snapchat and Periscope have been using vertical framing to create marketing content for mobile phones. Blurring the boundaries between amateur and professional media, these companies often encourage the production of user-generated vertical content alongside in-house and commissioned videos. This chapter argues that a shifting mobile media landscape (both technological and social) allows vertical framing to flourish and, in turn, problematises distinction between user-generated and corporate mobile media in the era of the smartphone.

Keywords Vertical video · Social media · Online video

D. Neal
Independent Researcher, Buena Vista, Colorado, USA

M. Ross (✉)
Victoria University of Wellington, Wellington, New Zealand

© The Author(s) 2018   151
M. Schleser and M. Berry (eds.), *Mobile Story Making in an Age of Smartphones*, https://Doi.org/10.1007/978-3-319-76795-6_15

While camera-enabled mobile phones have long allowed users to film and upload moving-image footage, it is only since 2012, when the Glove and Boots video "Vertical Video Syndrome—A PSA" became a viral hit, that widespread attention has been given to the way users are foregoing the traditional landscape orientation in favour of "vertical video". Glove and Boots' tongue-in-cheek video asked for an end to this phenomenon and sparked debate across social media with professional and semiprofessional practitioners coming to the consensus that vertical or portrait framing was inelegant, amateur and to be avoided (Canella 2017; Ross 2014; Ross and Glen 2014). Despite this consensus, there was continued uptake of vertically oriented filming and viewing. As noted by Mary Meeker in her twentieth Internet Trends report (2016), vertically oriented viewing on mobile devices increased from 5% of the time in 2010 to 29% in 2015, a sixfold increase. There was wide exposure to vertical videos on YouTube: 15.5 million views for "Buck has the hiccups", a short video of a puppy; 22 million views of "How to stop a baby from crying by Katy Perry Dark Horse" showing said baby reacting to music; 9.6 million views for "Guy annoys girlfriend with puns at Ikea", documenting a couple's visit to the furniture store; and 22.3 million views for "Hilarious Southwest flight attendant" depicting the humorous delivery of a safety announcement. These examples suggest a type of banality framed by the quotidian moments of the mobile phone user's life, placing them within the realm of vernacular media (Burgess 2006). However, vertical framing also gained more spectacular exposure when a number of celebrities—for example, Chris Pratt, Oprah Winfrey and Charlie Sheen—filmed themselves undertaking the Ice Bucket Challenge (a money-raising activity for charities dedicated to Amyotrophic Lateral Sclerosis) in 2014. In the same way that 'many of the subjects captured on camera phones are perhaps more associated with communicating aspects of personal experience with peers, rather than a preoccupation with "correct" framing, lighting and composition' (Keep 2014, pp. 17–18) the vertical framing and the low resolution of the Ice Bucket video footage emphasised a personal, authentic moment in which the celebrities' own mobile devices were used to capture them undertaking an activity that was performed in the same way by millions of people around the world.

As a signal of industry acceptance of the framing, YouTube released an update to its Android app in early 2015, allowing vertical videos to play full screen. It was quickly followed by an iOS upgrade. Although YouTube vertical videos had previously played full screen on many devices, the announcement by CEO Susan Wojcicki at the VidCon event demonstrated that major corporations were beginning actively to support vertical modes (Longwell 2015). This support for vertical framing coincided with a softening of attitudes across both traditional press and tech-oriented websites. For example, Farhad Manjoo at the New York Times noted: "to shoot vertically isn't to be exposed as a tech ignoramus or a lazy philistine who cares little for the creative process. Rather it is to be on the vanguard of a novel and potentially far-reaching artistic trend" (2015).

Also by 2015, a number of newer social media platforms, such as Snapchat and Periscope, began emphasising vertical framing for mobile. Operating in the arena of mobile apps, these platforms blur traditional conceptualisations of amateur and professional media by hosting user-generated content as well as in-house and/or commissioned work and marketing material in a virtual space where the distinction between them is often unclear. It is a continuation of the convergence between user-generated content and corporate environments that has already been noted across the internet (Deuze 2007; Dijck 2009), but a permutation that is taking place in a mobile-screen visual environment in which content is constantly reconfigured to match changing screen sizes and parameters. While we apply the term "user" in accordance with both literature in the field and terminology used by the platforms in their own marketing, this is not to suggest a passive consumer who is subject to the norms implemented by the platforms. Rather, users of these technologies produce media content in this arena with the same impetus as other makers described within this book, all the while negotiating the opportunities offered to them and how their work interacts with the porous definitions of amateur, prosumers and professional media. Following Hight's (2015) model for understanding user interaction in software studies, this chapter examines the shift in the mobile media landscape that allowed vertical modes to flourish, via both the affordances offered by technological support on new platforms and the interactions by users that demonstrated the value of this framing. In turn, it considers the implications vertical framing has for attempts to distinguish between user-generated and corporate mobile media content in the era of the smartphone.

Perhaps the largest platform for vertical footage outside of YouTube is Snapchat, an app that has grown from a simple peer-to-peer photo sharing app in 2011 (notorious for its ephemeral nature due to the deletion of content once viewed) to a content provider now offering dedicated entertainment and news in the form of "stories" (one-to-many messaging), "live stories" (curated many-to-many messaging) and "Discover" (professionally published news magazines, music videos and "shows"). Snapchat's support for vertical framing is narrated as a natural evolution by CEO Evan Spiegel in a video designed to promote Snapchat's use of a portrait orientation in its advertising content. Terming the advertising 3V (vertical, video, views), he states that it "is special because it is built from the ground up for mobile just like everything else on Snapchat" (Snapchat 2015). This suggests that the content is designed to match the pre-existent technological function of the mobile phone that increasingly encourages the user to hold the screen in a portrait orientation rather than follow the aesthetic norms of audio-visual media traditionally displayed on fixed horizontal screens. Snapchat's original photo-sharing design exemplified this process by making the capture, edit and sending of photographs as simple as possible for users accustomed to holding their smartphones vertically, leading to similar processes when video was introduced. This type of embodied "normalisation" of vertical framing counteracts arguments that moving-image content should only be framed horizontally while also registering a causal explanation, building on a platform of user-generated content: it suggests that Snapchat follows the users' needs and that human-centred desires drive a technological infrastructure.

The role of the mobile phone user in this context is, however, complicated by the way that Snapchat's own content, advertising and user-generated content are often blended. It becomes difficult to recognise, at least in the initial viewing stages, which videos and/or images are professionally produced, which are delivered by its users and which are advertising. It is a context that has already been taking place on platforms such as YouTube (Burgess and Green 2009) but is exaggerated by Snapchat's inner-facing app-only context whereby users must be registered in order to interact with content and there is an emphasis on connecting the quotidian experiences of its users. For example, Snapchat's "live story" concept mixes together footage from users with Snapchat's own camerawork to produce a story around a physical location (e.g. New York, London, Paris) and/or an event (e.g. Coachella, Burning Man, Bastille Day). These stories can then be branded in order to support corporate interest, as was seen in an early brand-based "story" called "SnapperHeros" that was sponsored by AT&T, produced by Billy Parks of Fullscreen, and featured a group of prominent YouTube and Snapchat users in a twelve-episode storyline. By making use of equipment such as iPhones in order to develop a "homemade" aesthetic, and then enhancing it with special effects, the boundaries between the production's visual designation as user-generated content and corporate product became porous in a similar manner to what has been happening with the iPhone as filming device over the last decade (Eriksson and Eriksson 2015; Goldstein 2012; Schleser 2014).

In Snapchat's other popular curated section, Discover, launched in January 2015, content is more clearly designated as professionally produced. Various media producers and outlets such as Comedy Central, the *Daily Mail*, National Geographic, CNN and BuzzFeed provide animated images and videos in short clips that then often link to full articles or interactive options. However, the news element in much of this content includes videos that appear to come from non-professional sources due to low-resolution images, shaky camerawork and/or low-quality audio. There is the potential for these clips to incorporate horizontally framed footage, but this footage is usually repurposed and augmented to fit within the assumed portrait orientation in which viewers will watch it. In each case, there is rarely an explicit acknowledgement that footage comes from amateur sources, but the vertical framing, along with the other aforementioned markers of non-professional filming technology, lends an air of authenticity, suggesting the large media producer companies are able to connect to and interact with real world events at the level of the everyday user (Ross 2014). The ephemeral nature of Snapchat's rapidly disappearing content means that individual items are rarely open to analysis and interrogation: even though Snapchat has increased the potential for users to save 'memories' and other contents in recent years, there is still not the same type of archiving processes in place that are applied to more traditional media. If anything, this extends the nature of ephemeral media that Paul Grainge (2011) saw increasing at the beginning of the twenty-first century, and the influence of this approach in the arena of social media apps is evidenced by the replication of this format across other platforms, particularly Facebook-owned Instagram (Mohan 2016). In this context, vertical framing has become a type of vernacular background practice that has the appearance of 'natural fit' rather than a configuration that is recognized as best serving the company's aim at speedy, proliferate and ubiquitous content.

Within this new distribution context there are strong avenues for the development of and recognition of "prosumers" as active creators of new audio-visual formats (Morreale 2014). These apps operate in similar ways to other audio-visual platforms that have highlighted an intensification of prosumer labour in the twenty-first century, particularly YouTube, which has become "the site of dynamic and emergent relations between market and non-market, social and economic activity" (Burgess and Green 2009, p. 90). And, like YouTube, prosumer "stars" have risen to the top (Postigo 2016), where "one index of this phenomenon is the extent to which performers with commercial ambitions and, at times, corporate sponsorship will use the cachet of the 'homegrown' and the 'grassroots,' predicated on their capacity to confer authenticity, to advance their budding careers" (Salvato 2009, p. 70). Whereas there are issues around the exploitation of the prosumer's labour in these contexts (Comor 2011; Deuze 2007; Fuchs 2010; Morreale 2014; Postigo 2016), it is notable that the prosumers monetising their efforts on these platforms are often able to do so because they circumvent traditional media success by adapting to the novelty of new technological interfaces. It is here that prosumers can use a vertical framing to project authenticity and sincerity, to use Nick Salvato's (2009) term, while gathering followers and views that can be used for monetary gains in partnership with the new apps. This is a shift from the widespread context in 2012 when prosumers articulated the superiority of horizontal over vertical framing to set themselves apart from "amateur" users (Ross 2014).

At the same time, there are still tensions between the affirmation and exploitation of the prosumer's labour and one of the areas where these are visibly played out is within the rapidly shifting landscape of news reporting. While the decline of print media has destabilised the role of news outlets and journalists in multiple ways, a particularly visible shift from the traditional one-way delivery of news to audiences is the use of user-generated videos in news stories, most frequently originating from cameras on mobile devices (Canella 2017). Vertical framing is common in these videos and, even when news outlets make use of a reverse pillarboxing technique to present blurry, colour-appropriate bars rather than black bars on the vertical edges of the image, the videos stand out as coming from beyond the production centre of traditional media. The opportunistic mobile phone user who happens to be at the scene of a newsworthy event, rather than the prosumer, is most likely to gain attention in this arena. However, with the uptake in news reporting in apps such as Snapchat, as well as the decision by traditional broadcasters such as the BBC to include vertical video in their news apps (Lichterman 2017), the boundaries between different content producers—the corporate pro-fessional, prosumer and everyday user—have, as with other contexts, become indistinct (Deuze 2007; Dijck 2009; Burgess and Green 2009). In Snapchat's Discover "news magazine", mentioned above, there is a blending of content, making it hard to discern which is produced by the news team and which comes from elsewhere. This is further con-fused by content from news organisations appearing across other parts of Snapchat. In September 2015, BBC News produced its first vertical video article on its Snapchat account, with an archival copy on Facebook (BBC News 2015). Beyond its use of vertical framing, the video bears many of the hallmarks of the Snapchat app through the use of rough, jump-cut edits, static images intercut with moving image footage and grey text placed on a black bar running horizontally across the screen. Without the BBC label, it could appear to be one of a large number of user-generated videos produced that month. In this case, one might say the professional is mimicking the prosumer and/or the everyday user, but the constant blending of content on the app means it is increasingly unclear who is doing the mimicking and whether mimicry is indeed tak-ing place.

One of the challenges for both the professional and prosumer using these apps (when aiming to monetise this use), however, is how to make content that fits the specificities of "built from the ground up for mobile" with the need to be able to utilise it on other platforms where a vertical format is not commonly accepted. As Kevin Roose, news direc-tor for *Fusion*, notes, "repackaging stories for Snapchat is harder than repackaging them for Facebook or Twitter, since it often requires custom animation, voice-over, and significant editing of the text itself" (2015, n.p.). More than this, a vertical frame offers a visually distinct space from horizontal framing, and so decisions about how to deal with frame ori-entation are imperative (Honigman 2016). As corporations continue to look for advertising and other monetising measures in the era of the smartphone they will have to be flexible in the way that they support content that responds to how users not only create but also view content in a variety of framings. At the same time, they will have to balance this with the impossibility of creating unique, new content for each differ-ent viewing platform. In this context, it is thus likely that the distinction between amateur and corporate content will continue to blur in order for corporations to exploit and maximise the activities of their prosum-ers and everyday users so that they can remain relevant and novel rather than traditional and potentially outdated. However, recognising the slippage between amateur and professional distinctions does not mean underestimating the agency users have to work these contexts in innovative and challenging ways. While literature in this area has pointed to separate roles—the corporate professional, prosumer and everyday user—the interventions that other chapters in this volume propose in order to understand mobile story-making open the field to understanding how a broader conceptualisation of the media "maker" allows users, as well as salaried staff working for corporate apps, to traverse these boundaries in complex ways. This facet makes it important to consider the extent to which seemingly vernacular practices such as framing in a vertical mode are carefully orchestrated within mobile media environments so that they can serve the interests of those that host them and the extent to which they offer productive avenues for makers to use mobile technologies, and the possibilities they afford, in new ways.

REFERENCES

BBC News. (2015). Following refugees around Europe, captured on Snapchat, by the BBC's John Sweeney. *Facebook*. Available at https://www.facebook.com/bbcnews/videos/vb.228735667216/10153126586842217/?type=2&theater [accessed 22 February 2017].

Burgess, J. (2006). Hearing ordinary voices: Cultural studies. *Vernacular Creativity and Digital Storytelling. Continuum, 20*(2), 201–214.

Burgess, J., & Green, J. (2009). The entreprenurial vlogger: Participatory culture beyond the professional-amateur divide. In P. Snickars & P. Vonderau (Eds.), *The Youtube Reader* (pp. 89–107). Stockholm: National Library of Sweden.

Canella, G. (2017). Video goes vertical: Local news videographers discuss the problems and potential of vertical video. *Electronic News*. Forthcoming.

Comor, E. (2011). Contextualizing and critiquing the fantastic prosumer: Power, alienation and hegemony. *Critical Sociology, 37*(3), 309–327.

Deuze, M. (2007). Convergence culture in the creative industries. *International Journal of Cultural Studies, 10*(2), 243–263.

Eriksson, P. E., & Eriksson, Y. (2015). Syncretistic images: iPhone fiction filmmaking and its cognitive ramifications. *Digital Creativity, 26*(2), 138–153.

Fuchs, C. (2010). Web 2.0, prosumption, and surveillance. *Surveillance & Society, 8*(3), 288–309.

Goldstein, T. (2012). *Hand held Hollywood's filmmaking with the iPad & iPhone*. Berkeley, CA: Peachpit Press.

Grainge, P. (2011). *Ephemeral media: Transitory screen culture from television to YouTube*. London: British Film Institute.

Hight, C. (2015). Software studies and the new audiencehood of the digital ecology. In F. Zeller, C. Ponte, & B. O'Neill (Eds.), *Revitalising audience research: Innovations in European Audience Research* (Vol. 5, pp. 62–79). New York: Routledge.

Honigman, B. (2016). The big flip: How Snapchat reoriented video advertising. *Business 2 Community*. Available at http://www.business2community.com/social-media/big-flip-snapchat-reoriented-video-advertising-01526591 [accessed 22 February 2017].

Keep, D. (2014). Artist with a camera-phone: A decade of mobile photography. In M. Berry & M. Schleser (Eds.), *Mobile media making in an age of smartphones* (pp. 14–24). Basingstoke: Palgrave Macmillan.

Lichterman, J. (2017). At the BBC, the launch of in-app vertical video is a step toward connecting with new audiences. *Nieman Lab*. Available at http://www.niemanlab.org/2017/01/at-the-bbc-the-launch-of-in-app-vertical-video-is-a-step-toward-connecting-with-new-audiences/ [accessed 25 August 2016].

Longwell, T. (2015). YouTube's Wojcicki reveals new mobile app, 360-degree 3D Support. *VideoInk*. Available at https://thevideoink.com/youtubes-wojcicki-reveals-new-mobile-app-360-degree-3d-support-ba36086a9a29 [accessed 22 February 2017].

Manjoo, F. (2015). Vertical video on the small screen? Not a crime. *The New York Times*. Available at http://www.nytimes.com/2015/08/13/technology/personaltech/vertical-video-on-the-small-screen-not-a-crime.html [accessed 25 December 2016].

Meeker, M. (2016). *2016 Internet trends report*. Available at http://www.kpcb.com/internet-trends [accessed 25 December 2016].

Mohan, P. (2016). Instagram stories is an exact copy of Snapchat stories. *Fast Company*. Available at https://www.fastcompany.com/4015702/instagram-stories-is-an-exact-copy-of-snapchat-stories [accessed 25 August 2016].

Morreale, J. (2014). From homemade to store bought: Annoying orange and the professionalization of YouTube. *Journal of Consumer Culture, 14*(1), 113–128.

Postigo, H. (2016). The socio-technical architecture of digital labor: Converting play into YouTube money. *New Media & Society, 18*(2), 332–349.

Roose, K. (2015). Snapchat discover could be the biggest thing in news since Twitter. *Fusion*. Available at http://fusion.net/story/47528/snapchat-discover-could-be-the-biggest-thing-in-news-since-twitter/ [accessed 26 December 2016].

Ross, M. (2014). Vertical framing: Authenticity and new aesthetic practice in online videos. *Refractory: A Journal of Entertainment Media, 24*. Available at http://refractory.unimelb.edu.au/2014/08/06/ross/.

Ross, M., & Glen, M. (2014). Vertical cinema: New digital possibilities. *Rhizomes, 26.* Available at http://www.rhizomes.net/issue26/ross_glen.html.

Salvato, N. (2009). Out of hand: You Tube amateurs and professionals. *TDR (1988–), 53*(3), 67–83.

Schleser, M. (2014). Connecting through mobile autobiographies: Self-reflexive mobile filmmaking, self-representation, and selfies. In M. Berry & M. Schleser (Eds.), *Mobile media making in an age of smartphones* (pp. 148–158). Basingstoke: Palgrave Macmillan.

Snapchat. (2015). *Introducing 3 V Advertising.* Available at https://www.youtube.com/watch?v=9JYZqg0511M [accessed 22 February 2017].

van Dijck, J. (2009). Users like you? Theorizing agency in user-generated content. *Media, Culture & Society, 31*(1), 41–58.

CHAPTER 16

Pasifika Youth and Health Perspectives: Creative Transformation Through Smartphone Filmmaking and Digital Talanoa

Max Schleser and Ridvan Firestone

Abstract Pacific people in New Zealand (NZ) have the highest rate of obesity (66%) in the world as defined by having a body mass index, BMI >30 kg/m^2, thus they experience a 30% higher incidence than the general population (33%) (Ministry of Health, Annual update of key results 2014/15: New Zealand health survey, 2015). In NZ, there is a critical need for effective, sustainable programmes that can be self-managed by indigenous communities in order to enable independent health and wellbeing and to reduce the prevalence of non-communicable diseases. Previous research programmes have shown that community-based and community-led programmes that are "fit for purpose" and relevant to the social–cultural environment are advantageous for

M. Schleser
Swinburne University, Melbourne, Australia

R. Firestone (✉)
Centre for Public Health Research, Massey University,
Wellington, New Zealand

© The Author(s) 2018
M. Schleser and M. Berry (eds.), *Mobile Story Making in an Age of Smartphones*, https://doi.org/10.1007/978-3-319-76795-6_16

161

improving the health and independent living of certain communities (Kaholokula et al. 2012b; Sinclair et al. in Annals of Behavioral Medicine: A Publication of the Society of Behavioral Medicine 45:24–32, 2013). The omnipresence of mobile, smartphone and wireless technologies provides an opportunity to explore new methods of engaging communities and sharing knowledge (Berry and Schleser 2014).

Keywords Community engagement · Story-making · Social impact

This interdisciplinary research combining public health, smartphone filmmaking and digital talanoa will use principles of the social change model in combination with creative engagement processes as a framework for empowerment. Empowerment programmes are educational-based programmes to build knowledge and skillsets in participants, enabling them to work towards a common goal (Morton and Montgomery 2011). For our work, the empowerment programme aimed to involve young people as partners in the decision-making process of a particular intervention. Documenting the changes from within the community through mobile-mentaries (mobile documentaries) (Schleser 2010) enables the participants to comment on changes in their lives. At an individual level, there is limited power to change the obesogenic environment. However, individuals and communities can be empowered to change their behaviours and advocate for wider changes. We developed the Pasifika Youth Empowerment Programme (YEP) involving youth aged 18–24 years from Wellington, New Zealand. The YEP project focuses on changing the mindset and cultural behaviours linked to obesity of a younger generation, empowering them through alternative health and lifestyle choices. The empowerment programme builds young people's capacity to address obesity-related issues that are culturally and personally relevant to them. As part of the mobile story-making process, smartphone filmmaking, social media and 360° videos were utilised.

HEALTH PERSPECTIVES IN AOTEAROA

Social–cultural perspectives are important when examining the determinants of health in Pacific peoples. The current assumption is that Pacific peoples do not share the same view of health as westerners

(Metcalf et al. 2000; Pollock 2001; Teevale 2011), and thus they may not view obesity as a health problem. The disparate issue here is the clash of definitions for, and understanding health from, a Pacific perspective. For instance, Pacific people may prioritise issues such as access difficulties, confidentiality, spiritual crisis, parenting, drugs and alcohol consumption as health issues because they impact on the wellbeing and lifestyle conditions of the family rather than body size and food portions (Final et al. 2003).

Pacific peoples migrated to New Zealand in the mid-1900s for "greener pastures", particularly in terms of better education and for optimistic economic opportunities. For Island-born people, difficulties in adapting to a new environment that was not aligned to traditional lifestyles was thought to be highly correlated with the high incidence of long-term conditions, such as obesity and diabetes (Final et al. 2003; Foliaki and Pearce 2003). The underlying challenge is to understand the role of a range of environmental risk factors including structural elements of inequality in society, stress of racism and discrimination (Nazroo 2003; Pickett and Wilkinson 2008) and others relating to the social distribution of resources (e.g. social support, interplay of family life and work) (Brown et al. 2009; Foliaki and Pearce 2003; Kaholokula et al. 2008, 2012a; Moore et al. 2003), and not just the socio-economic aspects, which have already been well documented (Brown et al. 2009; Foliaki and Pearce 2003; Metcalf et al. 2008; Ministry of Health 2012b; Schaaf et al. 2000; Statistics New Zealand and Ministry of Pacific Island Affairs 2010; Sundborn et al. 2006; Swinburn et al. 1997).

The prevalence of obesity among all New Zealand (NZ) adults aged 15+years is amongst the highest in the world, reaching 27% (Ministry of Health 2009); this means that NZ is ranked third amongst Organisation for Economic Co-operation and Development (OECD) countries, behind the United States of America (33.8%) and Mexico (30%). However, the highest burden of obesity in NZ is borne by Pacific peoples (Ministry of Health 2012a). The increasing prevalence of obesity over the last three decades suggests there has been little success in the development of interventions or programmes to address this disease effectively. Pasifika (defined here onwards as representing all Pacific Island nations from the South Pacific region) youth 16–24-year age group comprise 19% of the total Pacific population. This is an important age group, because these young people have the independence and capacity to understand their own and their families' social realities (Statistics New Zealand and Ministry of Pacific Island Affairs 2010).

This is also a critical age-window whereby the environment and social networks relating to the young people's cultural and social realities may have an important impact on pathways contributing to better (or poorer) health outcomes and lifestyle choices.

COMMUNITY ENGAGEMENT THROUGH CREATIVITY

The Pasifika Youth Empowerment Programme (YEP) is a project that aims to develop young people's public health knowledge and build leadership skills using an empowerment approach to improve healthy lifestyles, including nutritional habits, and to enhance health education and literacy, and physical activity. Empowerment programmes aim to build capacity in young people so that they become collaborative partners in the decision-making process when developing any preventative or intervention plans. By developing the capacity of Pasifika youth, we aimed to enrich their skills and knowledge base of public health relating to obesity and healthy lifestyles. By actively involving the youth in the research process, they became empowered to know, understand and ultimately feel motivated to make social changes or raise their community's awareness about healthy living. The principles of social change model (Astin and Astin 1996) underpins this research to develop the capacity of Pasifika youth to make important changes in their personal lives and those of their families and community.

We worked with fifteen Pasifika youth aged 18–24 years from Wellington, New Zealand. Their selection was based on a convenient sampling process. The youth who participated in the empowerment programme learned visual storytelling skills that can enrich their community beyond the duration of this programme. This approach was culturally relevant for the youth, as they verbally recorded their personalised stories using digitalised talanoa through the use of their personal smartphones and shared their stories with the other participants.

DIGITAL TALANOA

Intrinsic to the interdisciplinary research methods is the talanoa approach. "*Tala*" denotes holistic engagement between the research team and the participants. The process enlists emotions, knowledge and experiences that results in a synergy of connectedness and enlightenment. "*Noa*" is the social context and conditions where the encounter occurs, avoiding rigidity and challenges, and allows for flexibility (Voaioleti 2006). Talanoa is an appropriate Pacific research method for the project because it is based on a deep interpersonal relationship between the participants; thus it enhances the social conversation that can lead to critical reflections and discussions or creation of new ideas and knowledge resulting in rich contextual and inter-related information (Voaioleti 2006). Historically and traditionally, verbal exchange and interaction is how most Pacific activities are carried out (Morrison et al. 2002). By digitalising the talanoa process, the youth become more engaging within their environment (e.g. church, home), and the flexible use of their smartphones allowed for their stories to be more reflective, personalised, contextualised and meaningful, using their own voices.

MOBILE STORY-MAKING FOR PASIFIKA YOUTH

As part of a Pacific YEP, a workshop series was developed in synch with the talanoa approach. Three key sessions focused on mobile and smartphone storytelling, filming and editing. The concept of mobile-mentary (Schleser 2010), mobile documentaries, was further developed into a community-based approach. Within all sessions, a participatory framework was applied (Schleser 2010), in which filmmaker Max Schleser and Riz Firestone (public health researcher from Massey University) worked as facilitators to engage Pacific youth through the creative process of visual storytelling. Using a social media storytelling template (Schleser 2015) that was developed for a collaborative film project,[1] *#24Frames24Hours* (Schleser 2013–2015),[2] participants could reflect on their experience with healthy lifestyle alternatives. Participants created storyboards and then went out to film their contributions. The *#24Frames24Hours* story template provided a format for young people to work with so that they could craft their stories into mobile-mentaries. Once the filming was completed we worked in a communal and participatory editing session and collectively decided on how the individual stories would create a video that talks to young people. The video was disseminated using the Facebook group.[3] In alignment with the story-making approach, the dissemination of the work and creative practice of sharing the stories reflect the digital talanoa approach. Moreover, the bottom-up approach resulted in a meaningful video, *Pacific Youth (Mobile Storytelling)*, as young people can see themselves reflected with their vision being realised.[4]

A 2015 report on New Zealanders' use of smartphones and other mobile devices provided our creative approach with some interesting considerations. Over 90% of New Zealanders aged 18–34 own a smartphone and the daily use of all devices except for smartphones is trending downwards. According to statistics, YouTube, and even YouTube on mobile alone, reaches more 18–49-year-olds than any cable network in the USA.[5] More than half of YouTube views come from mobile devices and the average time spent on YouTube is forty minutes per day (YouTube 2016 online). One could consider concerns in this area on a number of socio-cultural levels beyond this study, but our objective of engaging with young Pacific youth meant that we had to develop a presence and feature content for social media that is most likely accessed by smartphones. By tapping into mobile-mentaries (Schleser 2010) and collaborative mobile filmmaking methods developed in earlier projects (Schleser 2012), we developed bottom-up creative strategies to develop meaningful messages for young people that mirror in form and content their personal mobile social media. The peer approach to production allowed us to ensure that the message becomes meaningful and authentic to the youth, whereby their friends are engaged in the process of making content. Therefore this bottom-up approach means that young people will relate to the content as they or their peers are part of the story, which is embedded in the idea of story-making. The 360° video approach enables us to get the full attention of our target audience, Pasifika youth, to the digital talanoa. The message, health perspectives and lifestyle alternatives are created by Pasifika youth for young Pasifika people.

Embracing 360° Video and Mobile VR

While the idea of Virtual Reality (VR) is not new and has been around since the 1990s (for example, 1991 Sega VR, 1994 Quicktime, VR Authoring Studio, 1995 Nintendo Virtual Boy and 2010 Oculus Rift), accessible omnidirectional video cameras that integrate with standard video production workflows (i.e. Adobe Premiere Pro) were launched in 2016 (for example, Go Pro Omi and Odyssey, Nokia OZO, Kodak Pixpro, Vuze Camera, Ricoh Theta and Samsung 360 gear). Humaneyes (producer of Vuze camera) believes that VR will "become a major communication platform" in a "VR echo system". Within the same timeframe one can perceive that recognition of the importance of participatory videos is now more common in the context of national and

commercial broadcasting (such as #MyEscape /Exodus our journey to Europe /#uploading_holocaust) or in digital marketing
(i.e. Google CCC brand guidelines); a shift from storytelling toward
story-making is recognisable. Google defines this as Create, Collaborate
and Curate. The process means that from conceptualisation the moment
of sharing is considered and becomes part of the story strategy (Larson
2015).[6] The second element that the project explored was the application of Google Cardboard glasses. Google Cardboard makes VR and
360° video possible in a community-based context. Hand in hand with
the emergence of 360° video production cameras, sometimes referred
to as "empathy machines" (Milk 2016), YouTube and Facebook introduced 360° video playback functionality. The interesting idea with 360°
video is that it provides a first touch point as a door to our story-world.
In an experience-driven (Pine and Gilmore 1999) and attention economy (Davenport and Beck 2002), 360° video ensures a passage for the
audience engagement. Following some key considerations outlined by
the Canadian Sharing in Health initiative, which bases its analysis on
Wired magazine, Kevin Kelly's knowledge management points are further developed for mobile story-making. This approach is further refer-
encing immediacy as a key aesthetic quality of mobile media (Schleser
et al. 2009). Personalisation is embedded in the young filmmaker's story
and her or his interpretation provides support and guidance for peers.
Its authenticity is one of the key values helping it tap into the young
people's mindset. As mentioned above, the mobile and CCC mobile story-making approach crystallised on making these digital stories accessible
and findable through a framework based on personal contacts and trust.
This, as a consequence, can lead to patronage and peer support.

CREATIVE TRANSFORMATION

The *Pacific Youth* video demonstrates opportunities for transforming the
health conscience of our Pasifika youth at an individual level. The mobile
and smartphone filmmaking workshop series developed the participants'
capacity in smartphone filmmaking and visual storytelling. Participants
filmed across various locations, capturing the diversity of daily activities
and contextualising their obesogenic environment (e.g. sports, shopping
at the food market). In a participatory editing session, the following elements were identified:

1. defining the YEP (what it is, who it targets and why);
2. the purpose of the YEP;
3. marrying the social–cultural perspectives from the past to the current health status of Pacific people in NZ today;
4. exploring the root causes of obesity;
5. how the YEP has transformed the youth participants; and
6. hopes and dreams for the future health of the next generation of Pacific people in NZ.

The YEP programme ended with a screening of the *Pacific Youth* video. A sense of achievement in terms of lifestyle and creative skill sets was celebrated. The final *Pacific Youth* video has been used across various settings. The clip has been shown to various stakeholders: (1) Pacific church communities; (2) researchers and academics at two international conferences (Pacific Health Gathering 2016, Fayetteville, Arkansas, USA; International Indigenous Health Symposium 2016, Honolulu, USA); (3) masters students in public health; (4) health workers at the Pacific Heartbeat Symposium 2016, Wellington, NZ (part of the NZ Heart Foundation and Pacific Heartbeat); (5) His Excellency Mr. Leasi Scanlan (Samoan High Commissioner, hosted by the youth in 2016, Massey University); and (6) mobile stakeholder representative (Mr. Juston Fenton) Samsung Electronics NZ. The observed impact from these settings has been positive and welcoming, with many communities and institutions requesting the YEP modules to be part of their existing programmes.[7]

Acknowledgements The research team would like to thank all participants who made each workshop a supportive and fun environment. A special thanks to Juston Fenton, Pre-Sales Solution Architect at Samsung Electronics New Zealand, for providing Gear 360 for the duration of the project. We would also like to acknowledge the Health Research Council of New Zealand (YEP project) and the Massey University Research Fund (Digital Diaries project) for the research funds.

NOTES

1. https://www.youtube.com/watch?v=Re5T1GXMVLU.
2. https://www.youtube.com/watch?v=zefqqRjY4to//http://www.24frames24hours.org.nz/.
3. https://www.facebook.com/AI-IA-E-OLA-Eat-To-Live-YEP-765024656946083.

4. https://www.youtube.com/watch?v=UgXs5L3UVYY.
5. YouTube (2016) online https://www.youtube.com/yt/press/statistics.html.
6. https://www.thinkwithgoogle.com/articles/building-youtube-content-strategy-lessons-from-google-brandlab.html.
7. Please feel free to contact Max Schleser Max@mina.pro for further information on mobile and smartphone filmmaking workshops.

Bibliography

Astin, H. S., & Astin, A. W. (Eds.). (1996). *A social change model of leadership development guidebook, version III*. The National Clearinghouse of Leadership Programs.

Berry, M., & Schleser, M. (2014). *Mobile media making in an age of smartphones*. New York: Palgrave.

Brown, D. E., Hampson, S. E., Dubanoski, J. P., Murai, A. S., & Hillier, T. A. (2009). Effects of ethnicity and socioeconomic status on body composition in an admixed, multiethnic population in Hawaii. *American Journal of Human Biology, 21*(3), 383–388. https://doi.org/10.1002/ajhb.20889.

Davenport, T., & Beck, J. (2002). *The attention economy: Understanding the new currency of business*. Brighton: Harvard Business Press.

Final, S., Tukuitonga, C., & Finau, E. (2003). *Health of Pacificans in Aotearoa*. Retrieved from Auckland.

Foliaki, S., & Pearce, N. (2003). Prevention and control of diabetes in Pacific people. *BMJ, 327*(7412), 437–439. https://doi.org/10.1136/bmj.327.7412.437.

Kaholokula, J. K., Grandinetti, A., Keller, S., Nacapoy, A. H., Kingi, T. K., & Mau, M. K. (2012a). Association between perceived racism and physiological stress indices in Native Hawaiians. *Journal of Behavioral Medicine, 35*, 27–37.

Kaholokula, J. K. A., Mau, M. K., Efird, J. T., Leake, A., West, M., Palakiko, D.-M., et al. (2012b). A family and community focused lifestyle program prevents weight regain in Pacific Islanders: A pilot randomized controlled trial. *Health Education & Behavior, 39*(4), 386–395. https://doi.org/10.1177/1090198110394174.

Kaholokula, J. K., Nacapoy, A. H., Grandinetti, A., & Chang, H. K. (2008). Association between acculturation modes and type 2 diabetes among Native Hawaiians. *Diabetes Care, 31*(4), 698–700.

Larson, K. (2015). https://www.thinkwithgoogle.com/marketing-resources/building-youtube-content-strategy-lessons-from-google-brandlab/ [accessed 1 October 2017].

Metcalf, P., Scragg, R., Willoughby, P., Finau, S., & Tipene-Leach, D. (2000). Ethnic differences in perceptions of body size in middle-aged European, Maori, and Pacific people living in New Zealand. *International Journal of Obesity and Related Metabolic Disorders, 24*(5), 593–599.

Metcalf, P., Scragg, R., Schaaf, D., Dyall, L., Black, P., & Jackson, R. (2008). Comparison of different markers of socioeconomic status with cardiovascular disease and diabetes risk factors in the diabetes, heart and health survey. *The New Zealand Medical Journal, 121*(1269), 45–56.

Milk, C. (2016). https://www.ted.com/talks/chris_milk_how_virtual_reality_can_create_the_ultimate_empathy_machine [accessed 1 October 2017].

Ministry of Health. (2009). Key facts and statistics on obesity in New Zealand.

Ministry of Health. (2012a). *A focus on nutrition: Key findings of the 2008/09 New Zealand adult nutrition survey.* Retrieved from Wellington.

Ministry of Health. (2012b). *A focus on Pacific nutrition: Findings from the 2008/2009 New Zealand adult nutrition survey.* Retrieved from Wellington.

Ministry of Health. (2015). Annual update of key results 2014/15: New Zealand health survey.

Moore, E., Owens, R. G., & Final, S. (2003). Health challenges of some urban Cook Island women in New Zealand. *Pacific Health Dialog, 10*(2), 16–26.

Morrison, S. L., Vaioleti, T. M., & Vermeulen, W. (2002). *Training for trainers in participatory learning in Samoa.* Retrieved from Apia, Samoa.

Morton, M., & Montgomery, P. (2011). Youth empowerment programmes for improving self-efficacy and self-esteem of adolescents. *Campbell Systematic Reviews, 5,* 79.

Nazroo, J. (2003). The structuring of ethnic inequalities in health: Economic position, racial discrimination, and racism. *American Journal of Public Health, 93*(2), 277–284.

Pickett, K. E., & Wilkinson, R. G. (2008). People like us: Ethnic group density effects on health. *Ethnicity & Health, 13*(4), 321–334.

Pine, J., & Gilmore, J. (1999). *The experience economy: Work is theatre & every business a stage.* Brighton: Harvard Business Press.

Pollock, N. (2001). Obesity of large body size? A study in Wallis and Futuna. *Pacific Health Dialog, 8*(1), 119–123.

Schaaf, D., Scragg, R., & Metcalf, P. (2000). Cardiovascular risk factors levels of Pacific people in a New Zealand multicultural workforce. *New Zealand Medical Journal, 113*(1102), 3–5.

Schleser, M. (2010). *Mobile-mentory mobile documentaries in the mediascape.* Doctoral thesis, University of Westminster. http://westminsterresearch.wmin.ac.uk/id/eprint/8877 [accessed 1 October 2017].

Schleser, M. (2012). Collaborative mobile phone film making. In E. Milne, C. Mitchell, & N. de Lange (Eds.), *Handbook of participatory video.* Blue Ridge Summit, PA, USA: AltaMira Press.

Schleser, M. (2013–2015). http://www.24frames24hours.org.nz/ [accessed 1 October 2017].

Schleser, M. (2015). https://www.youtube.com/watch?v=Re5T1GXMVLU [accessed 1 October 2017].

Schleser, M., Baker, C., & Kasia, M. (2009). Aesthetics of mobile media art. *Journal of Media Practice—Special Issue a Decade of Media Practice: Changes, Challenges and Choices, 10*(2 & 3), 100–122.

Sinclair, K. I. A., Thompson, C., Makahi, E. K., Shea-Solatorio, C., Yoshimura, S. R., Townsend, C. K. M., et al. (2013). Outcomes from a diabetes self-management intervention for Native Hawaiians and Pacific People: Partners in Care. *Annals of Behavioral Medicine: A Publication of the Society of Behavioral Medicine, 45*(1), 24–32. https://doi.org/10.1007/s12160-012-9422-1.

Statistics New Zealand, & Ministry of Pacific Island Affairs. (2010). *Pacific progress: Demographics of New Zealand's Pacific population.* Retrieved from Wellington.

Sundborn, G., Metcalf, P., Schaaf, D., Dyall, L., Gentles, D., & Jackson, R. (2006). Differences in health-related socioeconomic characteristics among Pacific populations living in Auckland, New Zealand. *The New Zealand Medical Journal, 119*(1228), 1–11.

Swinburn, B., Gillespie, A., Cox, B., Menon, A., Simmons, D., & Birbeck, J. (1997). Health care costs of obesity in New Zealand. *International Journal of Obesity and Related Metabolic Disorders, 21*(10), 891–896.

Teevale, T. (2011). Body image and its relation to obesity for Pacific minority ethnic groups in New Zealand: A critical analyses. *Pacific Health Dialog, 17*(11), 33–53.

Voaioleti, T. (2006). Talanoa research methodology: A developing position on Pacific research. *Waikato Journal of Education, 12,* 21–34.

INDEX

© The Editor(s) (if applicable) and The Author(s) 2018
M. Schleser and M. Berry (eds.), *Mobile Story Making in an Age
of Smartphones*, https://doi.org/10.1007/978-3-319-76795-6

GPSR Compliance

The European Union's (EU) General Product Safety Regulation (GPSR) is a set of rules that requires consumer products to be safe and our obligations to ensure this.

If you have any concerns about our products, you can contact us on

ProductSafety@springernature.com

In case Publisher is established outside the EU, the EU authorized representative is:

Springer Nature Customer Service Center GmbH
Europaplatz 3
69115 Heidelberg, Germany